TOM
HIDDLESTON

TOM HIDDLESTON

THE BIOGRAPHY

NAIMA CORSANI

JOHN BLAKE

Published by John Blake Publishing Ltd,
3 Bramber Court, 2 Bramber Road,
London W14 9PB, England

www.johnblakebooks.com

www.facebook.com/johnblakebooks 🅵
twitter.com/jblakebooks 🅴

This paperback edition published in 2017

ISBN: 978 1 78606 267 3

British Library Cataloguing-in-Publication Data:

A catalogue record for this book is available from the British Library.

Design by www.envydesign.co.uk

Printed in Great Britain by CPI Group (UK) Ltd

1 3 5 7 9 10 8 6 4 2

Papers used by John Blake Publishing are natural, recyclable products made
from wood grown in sustainable forests. The manufacturing processes
conform to the environmental regulations of the country of origin.

Every attempt has been made to contact the relevant copyright-holders,
but some were unobtainable. We would be grateful if the
appropriate people could contact us.

John Blake Publishing is an imprint of Bonnier Publishing
www.bonnierpublishing.co.uk

CONTENTS

CHAPTER ONE

EARLY DAYS

It must be every parent's ambition to give his or her child a head start in life, setting them up emotionally, intellectually and financially for the years ahead. Drawing on a lifetime of earned experiences, ageing adults hope their energetic offspring will not only match their own achievements, but better them – realising long-held dreams with the benefit of youthful enthusiasm.

The Hiddleston family was no different.

An enthusiastic new father, James Norman Hiddleston hoped his brood would have access to the best opportunities in life. His ambitions were made greater by his own humble upbringing. Born in Glasgow, he'd grown up in a working-class environment. His father was employed by the local shipyard and worked long hours to earn enough money to feed his family. The work was physically draining and often tough. From very early on, James knew this was a life he didn't want to repeat. He had much bigger dreams and he knew his only escape route came in the form of education.

Determined to break away from the social confines set by earning power and an antiquated British class system, he put every ounce of his energy into study. While his friends were out kicking footballs in rubbish-strewn backstreets or skipping classes to smoke sneaky cigarettes behind the bike sheds, James was brushing up on his arithmetic and reading feverishly in an effort to improve his vocabulary.

In his teens he landed a job in a local butcher's. The extra cash would help pave the foundation for his future studies. Between the classroom and workplace he also managed to fit in time to do his homework. He was often exhausted, but knew there was no time to rest: commitment and diligence underpinned his persona.

His efforts paid off. Following a stint at the local grammar school, he earned himself a place at Newcastle University. By all accounts James Hiddleston was a self-made success story. Hunger and fierce determination had enabled him to secure a foothold on a social ladder that had always seemed beyond reach. Now the future ahead of him suddenly seemed much brighter.

Despite these advances he never once looked down on his parents. After all, they had dedicated their lives to caring for their family. In those days it had been about day-to-day survival: earning enough money to put food on the table was the goal. But the world was changing. A new middle class was fast emerging and with it ambitions were growing. James Hiddleston was part of a new generation, but he would never forget his past. That was one lesson greater than any learned in the classroom, which he was keen to pass down to his own children.

At the extreme opposite end of the spectrum Diana Patricia Servaes had a very different upbringing. The descendent of several military greats, with roots in England, Wales and Germany, her family tree gleamed with honours and medals. As her contemporaries would say, she came from 'good stock'. Her grandfather, Ronald Vestey, had been a vice admiral in the British Navy, a fact the family recounted with immense pride, and her great grandfather was Sir Edmund Hoyle Vestey, chairman of the Blue Star Line, one of the great shipping companies. The Vestey family seat is 6,000-acre Stowell Park estate in the Cotswold Hills in Gloucestershire.

Along with wealth, Diana would also inherit an appreciation of the arts and culture. Alongside her studies, she learned to play the organ, a hobby she would continue into later life. Her parents ran the prestigious Aldeburgh Festival. She grew up on a diet of opera and theatre so it was perhaps inevitable that she would end up doing a job connected to those fields. She trained as a stage manager, a career that would allow her to immerse herself in the world she loved.

On paper, James Hiddleston might not have appeared to be her ideal suitor, but this working-class Scot with great ambitions was the man who eventually charmed and married her.

The couple both lived in London and decided to set up home together in Wimbledon, a leafy suburb in the capital's southwest. The theatres and playhouses of the West End were within easy reach, yet the smoke and pollution of the busy city centre was far enough removed. Following the birth of their first child, a girl they named Sarah Alexandra, in 1979, Diana fell pregnant with a boy. Thomas William Hiddleston was born on 9 February 1981.

Reaping the rewards of a well-spent youth, James was earning a reasonable income. His salary allowed his wife to give up work and concentrate all her efforts on motherhood. Diana would stay at home and play music to her children.

'I have a very happy memory,' recalled Tom years later, when talking about his childhood. 'My mum used to play the piano for me and my older sister when we were very, very small, about three or four.

'There was no furniture in the living room of the new house that we had moved into so my sister and I would dance around the living room. It's one of my earliest memories and it's a very happy one. I was just dancing to my mum playing the piano and she had these three things she used to play.'

There were times when Diana missed the buzz of the theatre world. Following a stint as an arts administrator, she had landed a job as a casting director for an opera company but after some discussion with her husband, she decided it was time to divert her attention to a far more rewarding career. After Tom, she gave birth to a second daughter, Emma Elizabeth, in 1986. Looking after the family became a full-time occupation.

Meanwhile things were looking up for James. In the early nineties he was offered a position as managing director of a pharmaceutical biotechnology company with links to Oxford University and so it was decided the family would pack up their belongings and relocate to Oxford.

James found the prospect of the new role incredibly stimulating, acting as a point of connection between the worlds of business and academic science. The salary was equally appealing, and allowed him to give Sarah, Tom and Emma the best education possible. Of course he would make sure his children didn't take anything for granted and constantly reminded them of his own humble upbringing, emphasising just how lucky they were to have such opportunities. He was determined to give them the best educational foundation possible for whatever career they chose to pursue in later life.

Diana, meanwhile, was channelling her creative energies into her children. In particular, her son, Tom, had developed a fondness for theatre. It was an interest she was eager to nurture. Tom and his sisters were forever inventing plays and acting out different roles.

'When I was a child my sisters and I and my cousins used to write plays in the summer for my parents,' he later recalled. 'This was in the years before Xbox and PlayStation and all that stuff so we just wrote and we just played. And at the end of the summer, we'd perform them for our parents. It always felt like such a huge deal, but it was literally five people and a dog in the audience in the back garden. There was one amazingly innovative one when I look back on it, and it didn't come from me.

'There was one called *TV Travelers*, which was about two kids watching TV and they get pulled in and it's kind of like *Dungeons & Dragons* or *The Purple Rose of Cairo*. And suddenly, they were traveling around in the world of the TV, which we thought was hugely creative at the time. And we did a version of *Cinderella*. It was very innocent and really cool.

'That's when I started acting. My sisters and my eldest cousin, Zoe, would write the play. My cousin Matt would make the stage. He was really good with his hands, so he'd make swords, a ship, the sea and all that stuff. I was always the bad guy for some reason. I guess nothing's changed. I think I'm pretty sure I played Hook at one point; we did our own version of *Peter Pan*, which I think involved the swimming pool. My cousins had a swimming pool and we were on holiday.'

As a child, Tom loved to read fantasy fairy tales and he was a huge fan of the Disney films. He later said: 'I grew up on *Peter Pan*. I grew up on J.M. Barrie's book and the Disney film. It was one of the films that me and my sisters – and my whole family – used to watch on a loop. We grew up on all of those early Disney movies, including *The Jungle*

Book, Peter Pan, Sleeping Beauty, Robin Hood and *Mary Poppins*, which is one of my favourite films.

'I loved the story of Neverland… and the story of the Lost Boys and the pirates, as well as Tinker Bell and Wendy. I loved all that stuff. Later, we'd watch *E.T.* together and *Indiana Jones* and *Star Wars* and *Dirty Dancing* and *Uncle Buck* and basically all those movies of the '80s that any child of the '80s grew up on!'

With hindsight, he believes having a fertile imagination at such a young age was instrumental in shaping his acting skills:

'Whether it's cowboys and Indians or Obi-Wan Kenobi and Darth Vader, you just play out whatever's in your imagination,' he added.

From very early on, it was clear Tom could be an entertainer. Years later, his sisters would pull together a reel of footage featuring his antics. 'It was from 1986 to 1994,' he recalled in an interview with *Industrial Insider* in 2014 'which my dad had taken with his old VHS home camera, as they were, or "Home Entertainment Systems" as they were called, I think, and it was really startling how much of a show-off I was as a child.

'I was always, forever, doing impressions and doing voiceovers of trailers of a family holiday in Canada.

'I had two very shy cousins, and I would go and stay with them and they would say "Be funny, Tom" and I would do a little show for them.'

Occasionally, though, his antics would get him into trouble.

'Once, my cousin and I thought it would be fun to hide underneath our beds at bath time,' he told the *Huffington Post* in 2014. 'We were four or five years old, and we were in the middle of a game, so we didn't want to sit in the bath. We stayed there for hours, but we decided to come out when my aunt picked up the phone to call the police. I'm generally well behaved now, but that was 25 years ago. That's the sort of thing you do when you're five, right?'

Little did Diana know that, years later her son would be one of Hollywood's biggest names, receiving plaudits from the likes of Sir Kenneth Branagh and Woody Allen. For now, he was simply a bright boy who was interested in film and theatre, and she regarded it as her duty to introduce him to the finest works, steering clear of mainstream blockbusters and focusing instead on quality material.

'She loved it [the theatre], and she recognised that I loved it as well, which made it a very special thing to share,' recalled an adult Tom Hiddleston, when reflecting on his childhood introduction to the arts.

Indeed the Hiddleston clan would regularly make trips to the RSC in Stratford and the National Theatre in London. Diana would often choose the productions, knowing her open-minded children would be receptive to her suggestions.

'When I was in my teens, she was always the one to suggest possibly going to the Picturehouse [arthouse cinema] rather than the Odeon,' says Tom with pride. 'So she was always peppering my appetite for *Jurassic Park* and

Terminator 2 with an appetite for [Michael Winterbottom's] *Jude* or whatever.'

As he grew older, several productions would have a big impact on his life. One of his favourites was Richard Eyre's 1996 production of Ibsen's *John Gabriel Borkman*, starring Paul Scofield; he would later describe it as 'an epiphany'. Other influences include Trevor Nunn's 1997 National Theatre production of Ibsen's *An Enemy of the People*, starring Ian McKellen, and Sam Mendes's 1997 version of *Othello*, starring Simon Russell Beale. Of the latter Hiddleston says: 'I saw that three times!'

Through shared artistic interests, Diana forged a strong relationship with her only son. James also developed a deep-rooted connection, although the male bond was formed in a more stereotypical way: the pair would often sit down to watch a rugby match together.

'When Scotland played England, I would support Scotland with him,' reveals Tom, who developed a deep respect for his father. 'My dad made himself from the ground up,' he says proudly. He was well aware that James had 'come from nothing' and had tried his hardest to give his children 'the best education'.

Tom knew his parents came from very different worlds but he believed those differences were a strength. 'I'm an inheritor of so many different parts of the British experience,' he would later joke. Although both his parents were 'very curious people', they always had their offspring's interests at heart. 'I feel as much defined by their tastes and their complexities as anything else,' Tom proudly admitted to the *Evening Standard* in 2013.

James's hard work ethics and ambitions would shape Tom's own personality, while Diana's passion for theatre and culture was infectious. But above all, it was their love and attention that he truly cherished.

'I feel so grateful to my mother and father for a happy childhood,' he would explain to journalists many years later in adult life. 'There are things I now understand that they were able to give me that are very special. And I think the early years, the first decade of your life, is the most formative in a way.'

Those first ten years would certainly help map out Tom Hiddleston's future. In years to come he would be performing on the stage rather than sitting in the audience. He would recite the works of playwrights he'd admired for many years, and would eventually become a household name.

All that, though, was yet to come; for now, the young Hiddleston had to concentrate on getting a good education.

CHAPTER TWO

AN EDUCATION

James Hiddleston only ever wanted the best for his family, particularly when it came to education. He saved enough money to pay for private schools and enrolled Tom into Oxford's Dragon School, a co-educational boarding and day establishment.

Building on the combined intellect of his mother and father, Tom was quick to learn and sailed through his studies so it came as no surprise when he secured a place at Eton College, the prestigious boarding school where countless politicians and even members of the royal family have been taught.

James went to have a look around the school grounds and came back brimming with enthusiasm. Both staff and grounds had really impressed him; it was just as he'd imagined. Unable to contain his excitement, he told Tom:

'There were 15 football pitches. Can you imagine? Fifteen. Amazing. There's a theatre with its own lighting rig. There's a building just for painting. You have to go. Have to.'

Walking through the hallowed corridors of the grand building made the awe-struck 13-year-old's chest swell with pride. Along with having access to excellent teachers and study material, he would also be keeping great company. A year after Tom joined, Prince William joined the year below. But Tom dismisses stereotypes of Eton as an establishment designed exclusively for rich and famous students. In fact, he would later claim quite the opposite was true.

'It's actually one of the most broadminded places I've ever been,' he revealed many years later to the *Daily Mail*. 'The reason it's a good school is that it encourages people to find the thing they love and to go for it. They champion the talent of the individual and that's what's special about it.'

Although Prince William was also attending classes, Tom never actually had the opportunity to become acquainted with the future heir to the throne.

'He seems like a genuinely well-adjusted man,' Tom told *GQ* magazine. 'But I feel as remote from or as close to him as you do.'

In reality, Eton treated members of royalty just as they would the grandson of a butcher from Glasgow – both students were judged on their merits. 'There was a general and very quietly stated ethos when he arrived that there was to be no special treatment and no special favours,' says Tom of Prince William.

'It would have made everyone's life hell if they had to treat him as someone special. I think it was very healthy for him to be just another boy.'

Although Tom didn't get the chance to forge a bond with the Prince, he did develop many other long and lasting friendships. Days off were spent listening to music, 'meeting girls, playing sport' and generally behaving like a regular teenager. Back then Radiohead, Oasis and Blur were three of the bands regularly played on the stereo.

Tom says of Eton: 'I have very, very good friends that I made there, but just like anyone, the friends that you make when you're growing up are the people who really know you.' Looking back, he adds: 'I thoroughly enjoyed my time. There's this idea of immovable structure and tradition, where rules remain in place from hundreds of years back, but instead there's a freedom and an encouragement for self-exploration. I like dispelling the generally held beliefs because, more often than not, they are totally inaccurate. I discovered who I wanted to be while I went there.'

Everyone would always refer to him by his surname, he recalled. 'It was always "Hiddleston this, Hiddleston that. Hiddleston, are you coming to class? Hiddleston, quit daydreaming". The teachers, the other boys... It's so odd now, I don't think anyone has called me anything else other than Tom since then. It's a strangely odd phenomenon that we all go through, particularly boys, I guess. You become so conditioned to it and then you leave, go to university, make your way in life and suddenly, that all ends.'

As a young child, Tom recalls being 'intermittently quiet and playful'. It's true, at times he was very introspective but his behaviour never displayed any signs for great concern. In many ways he was much more mature than his contemporaries. He would spend far longer reflecting on situations and analysing events.

'I was always concerned about wasting time,' he admits. 'I don't ever want to look back and think: "Why wasn't I doing something or making something?"' As a result, he used his time wisely, reading books, going to the theatre and learning new things. He also developed a rather odd fascination with reading obituaries.

'I used to read obituaries obsessively. They always started with a birth date and maybe the county where the subject was raised — and then the life would start at 25. What happened to those 25 legitimate years of good living time?' he told the *Evening Standard*.

Although the young Tom Hiddleston had several good friends, he was generally lacking in confidence and preferred to hide in the shadows rather than be the centre of attention. But his time spent at boarding school forced him to be more outspoken and to trust both his judgements and instincts. Soon he was no longer afraid to speak up in lessons or to defend his opinion in debates.

'I went to boarding school when I was seven and then I sort of learned how to deal with it. I was very vulnerable at first,' he admits.

Initially, he missed his parents and his siblings and home

comforts. Indeed the idea of spending so much time in the company of strangers also made him feel uneasy. But with time, he learned to share his space with others. Phone calls home also helped him to settle down. He thought long and hard about how much time and effort his father had invested in his education and was determined to make him proud. Whenever he spoke to his parents, he always made an effort to be positive and to tell them about all the new things he'd learned. 'I must have somehow got more independent through that experience,' he says. 'I've never sort of had analysis about this or anything, so I have no idea, but you just kind of move on.'

Although initially challenging, the experience of being away from home for the first time was by no means negative. 'It wasn't damaging, but I'm sure it made me independent,' he says proudly.

A far greater conflict in Hiddleston's young life came when his parents announced they were getting divorced. At the time he was just thirteen – old enough to understand the implications of the separation but still young enough to yearn for the security of a happy family life.

It's hard for any child when a marriage falls apart. Tom was a sensitive and introspective soul and he would spend hours mulling over in his head how such a thing could have happened. Deep inside, he wished there was something he could do to make things better but the decision had been made: James and Diana would go their separate ways. For decades to come James would remain at the family home in Oxford, while Diana was to start a new life elsewhere. Eventually she would end up in the Suffolk town of Aldeburgh, where her parents used to run the famous local festival, and she would embark on a new career as a freelance arts consultant.

Both parents agreed their children's happiness was now their main priority and did everything to reassure Tom and his two sisters that they still loved them very much and would be ever present in their lives.

'I like to think it made me more compassionate in my understanding of human frailty,' Tom would later say of that time. 'It was very difficult and I always say that it made me who I am, because it made me take responsibility for my life and I saw my parents for the first time as human beings, not as perfect love machines.

'They were both very badly hurt. I mean, it's hard enough when you're ending a short-term relationship, isn't it? I can't imagine what it's like to end a 17-year marriage!' he told the *Independent*.

At thirteen, though, Tom was still very confused and it would take him several years to come to terms with the collapse of a marriage he'd always naively believed, like so many children, might last forever. For the first time he realised his parents weren't perfect. All of a sudden everything he'd held dear in life was starting to collapse around him. He began to doubt everything. But more than anything, he felt sad. It was terrible to see two people he loved so much having to endure so much pain and suffering.

The last thing he wanted was to add to their pressures. Instead, he looked for new ways to release his emotions. He found solace in a somewhat unusual place – the school drama room.

'I think I started acting because I found being away at school while my parents were divorcing really distressing,' he explained to the *Daily Mail* with hindsight.

'It's only now I've got a retrospective angle on it. When you are a teenager, suddenly you start harbouring secrets in a different way. If you are at a boys' school, especially, there is a level of bravado that you have to keep up otherwise you'll get picked on. I was really quite upset, and probably very sad and vulnerable and angry. Acting presented a way of expelling those feelings in a safe place.'

By pretending to be someone else for a few hours Tom could easily forget his troubles. 'As a teenager, you're developing these more sophisticated feelings and attitudes about the world, but you don't have the language to express them,' he says. 'Plays gave me the articulacy to express what I was thinking.'

Looking back, though, he refuses to draw any direct links between his parents' divorce and the spark of an acting career. In his book life simply isn't that black and white; the way everything panned out certainly isn't the direct result of one single event. 'Events in anyone's life become these coat hangers on which you can hang your identity, and I'm wary of reinforcing the infrastructure of those things. It's only retrospectively that you join the dots up. Life is so much more accidental than any of us like to imagine,' he insists.

As a young man, he simply felt attracted to the stage. After swapping the rugby field for the drama studio his attention was diverted away from sport and into an exciting world of arts and culture where he began to appreciate the many playwrights and novelists his mother had enthusiastically introduced him to as a child. He also recalled being singled out in those early days by his teachers as someone with a special talent for acting: 'The weird thing about serious acting is I've always done impressions of people, all my life, and I did this thing called a balloon debate,' he revealed in an interview with website *Just Jared* in 2011.

'The idea is there's a hot air balloon traveling across the Atlantic and it's going down and you have to give a speech as to why you should stay in the balloon.

'Six people are going to be chucked out and you want to stay. You can choose who you are so people would choose, like, Einstein or the man who invented the wheel, the President of the United States, Shakespeare, Mozart, whoever it happens to be, you could pick these fun people, and I chose to be some kind of TV commercial actor, which basically meant that I could, for half an hour, do impressions of all the popular TV commercials at the time.

'And the head of drama came up to me after that and said, "You know, you have something quite unique, do you fancy being in the school play?" And that's how I got into it, just messing around with TV commercials. Never told anybody that.'

One of Tom's early performances was alongside flame-haired Eddie Redmayne, who would later soar to fame as Newt Scamander in *Fantastic Beasts and Where to Find Them* (2016), part of the *Harry Potter* franchise. But for now the two young men were simply two well-educated young boys auditioning for school plays.

Later Tom would reveal to journalists that he'd starred alongside Eddie in a school production of E.M. Forster's *A Passage To India*. He had been the leg of an elephant on which Eddie had sat. 'One of my finest hours,' he joked. Fortunately, he started to land much more significant roles after his drama teachers realised he had a talent.

Eddie Redmayne later described his former classmate as being 'fantastic' in a performance of Tom Stoppard's *Arcadia*, in which he played Bernard Nightingale. Around this time, Tom also deepened his interest and appreciation for Shakespeare: 'I saw Simon Russell Beale in Sam Mendes's 1998 *Othello* and I thought he was astonishing. I was 17 years old and I understood Shakespeare to be dry and just words on a page, but Simon spoke the words as if he wasn't making it up. It was thought-provoking and I couldn't believe it was Shakespeare – at that point I realised his plays needed to be performed, not just read.

'I also vividly remember Baz Luhrmann's 1996 *Romeo + Juliet*. I was 15 years old – the target audience for that film – and it had such a profound effect on me. I now cannot watch *Romeo + Juliet* without thinking about that film – I can't separate the two,' he told *Harper's Bazaar* in 2014.

Rather than pursue a conventional career, teachers hinted the young Hiddleston might want to consider taking up acting in the future. Encouraging compliments and words of praise would provide a solid foundation for his later career.

'The drama department is amazing and they really believed in me and I guess that's my blessing,' enthuses Tom. 'A bunch of people were unafraid of saying, "You could probably go off and do this for a living", which is quite unconventional in terms of what people associate with that place. Eton is famous for churning out investment bankers and Conservative politicians.'

By the time Tom was eighteen he'd fallen passionately in love with the stage. A real turning point came when he was cast in a production of *Journey's End*, an R.C. Sherriff play about World War I. The show played at the Edinburgh Festival in 1999, and received glowing reviews.

'*Journey's End* itself is an extraordinary play,' explained Tom, 'because it's set in a trench with a group of public school educated officers who have graduated from being captain of the rugby and the cricket team to being captain of the company, leading a company or a battalion of men across no-man's-land to fight the Germans.'

He praised the production for being 'very well staged': 'Everybody was impeccably cast and, somehow, without too much effort, we created a very classic production which became a huge hit at that festival. And it surprised me because I wasn't particularly reaching for it.'

The entire Hiddleston clan was in the audience and was overwhelmed by Tom's performance. For the first time they realised his acting potential. 'Mum and Dad [and] my sisters came and they all said, independently, that they'd never seen me do anything like that,' he says, beaming with pride.

'They said: "This is a bit different, what you're doing now; this isn't just showing off, this is communicating something deep and profound and you were amazing in it." And I had such a good time, as well.'

More than anything he has been eager to please his parents and he hoped they would share his enthusiasm for acting: 'I was 18 and it was the first time that people I knew and loved and respected came up to me after the show and said, "You know, you could really do this if you wanted to."

'Acting takes such a level of confidence and self-belief and as a teenager I didn't have that much self-esteem. What teenager does? It was when they started saying I could do it that I really committed to it as a possibility.'

Although in his heart Tom dreamed of a career in acting he was determined not to forget his studies. His father had worked so hard to provide the best future for his son and he didn't want to let him down. Throughout his school years his grades were excellent and his teachers also praised him for his polite nature and sharp intellect. After studying hard for A levels he scored straight As in Latin, Greek,

English and Theatre Studies so it came as no surprise when he was offered a place at Cambridge University to study Classics. Of course James and Diana were thrilled when he announced the news.

Just before Tom was about to leave Eton, he received a note from one of his drama teachers, Charles Milne, who had always been extremely complimentary about his star pupil: 'I was just about to go to Cambridge, and he wrote me a card afterwards that said: "Go to Cambridge and enjoy it. Jump in and enjoy the ride, the experience of it. But maybe on the other side, think about being an actor." And those moments where someone bolsters your self-belief like that, they are very, very rare.'

CHAPTER THREE

THE ACTING CRAFT

A long with Oxford, Cambridge is considered to be one of the world's best universities. In addition to its academic reputation, it is almost equally famous for a thriving arts scene and the Cambridge Footlights.

Tom had enrolled at Pembroke College and he couldn't wait to start his degree in Classics, a subject that had always interested him. Equally appealing was the university's amateur dramatic club. He quickly signed up and expressed great interest in being involved in future projects.

'Cambridge University is world-famous for its production of directors and actors, of all kinds, and comedians, and I knew there was a scene for that and the first thing I did was I found the acting community and got myself involved,' Tom told *Industrial Insider* in 2014.

He would be keeping great company. After a few weeks

he realised the calibre of students was extremely high and the competition for landing lead roles would be fierce. But no matter – he was simply happy to be in such good company. There was so much to learn and he was keen to soak up as much information and experience as possible.

'I love the acting community at Cambridge,' he enthuses, looking back on his university days. 'It's really quite committed and serious, since the days of Derek Jacobi and Ian McKellen right through to Emma Thompson and Hugh Laurie.'

While most of his Eton school friends had gone to Oxford because 'it seemed more of an easy bridge', Tom was pleased with the choice he'd made. Getting a place, though, wasn't easy. Even though the bright young pupil also had the right credentials, the examiners made sure to put him through his paces. There had been lots of negative news in the press suggesting Oxford and Cambridge were elitist establishments and so the university board had to ensure everyone was admitted based purely on their ability, regardless of wealth and status.

Contrary to the many stereotypes abounding, Cambridge actually attracted a mixed bag of students from a variety of countries and backgrounds. Tom revelled in the diversity and enjoyed meeting people with different stories to tell.

'Cambridge is a meritocratic place,' he says. 'I know this sounds odd, but I met more kinds of people there than I've probably met in any place in my life. It seemed to be so international, and there were people from all walks of life, all backgrounds.'

Later on in his career, some unkind critics would make jibes at Hiddleston for his privileged education. In reality, he didn't receive any special treatment. His tutors knew he was bright, but constantly sought to challenge him and would chastise him if they ever thought he was underperforming. Studying was hard work and demanded focus and attention: 'They made sure I was able to think for myself and stand on my own two feet, intellectually. Any chips on any shoulders had to be very swiftly removed.'

Given his private school background it would be all too easy to label Tom arrogant or over-confident, although he was actually a very humble student. 'I'm always distrustful of inherited confidence and inherited esteem,' he says. 'I've never wanted to have to transfer the credit for my actions on to anybody else – my parents, my school, my university. I've always understood an inherited confidence to be false.'

Very quickly lecturers and students alike identified Hiddleston as the undergraduate most likely to succeed. But he was sensible enough to divide his time carefully between rehearsing for theatre productions and writing essays, although he secretly yearned to spend longer on stage. He even managed to perform a role entirely in Ancient Greek, in the university's annual Greek play in October 2001, when he played the male lead, Orestes, in Sophocles' *Electra* at the Cambridge Arts Theatre.

Diana was extremely supportive of her son's acting

ambitions. With her background in the arts it had always been her dream that one day one of her children would craft a career in a realm she so dearly loved. Tom would regularly speak to his mum and update her on the latest scripts he was reading. She always told him to follow his heart. However, his father James wasn't quite so convinced. Although he enjoyed watching Tom's performances and could clearly recognise his talents, he was sceptical about acting as a career choice. As far as he was concerned his son clearly had a fine brain and it would be a waste not to use it. Given his excellent grades, he could land any number of high-flying positions.

'My father and I used to tussle about me becoming an actor. He's from strong, Presbyterian Scottish working-class stock,' admits Tom.

On one occasion, while visiting Tom, James decided it was his responsibility to raise his doubts. He sat his son down and said: 'You know, 99 per cent of actors are out of work. You've been educated, so why do you want to spend your life pretending to be someone else when you could be your own man?'

After all, Tom was a bright lad. Surely he'd lose interest in such a shallow career path after a few years? He needed something more stimulating to challenge him.

Although they had several arguments over the matter, Tom did appreciate his father's concern. While he didn't agree with his opinion he understood why James thought that way. Growing up, he'd always worked hard and his goal had been to get a good salary to earn enough money to take care of his family. Surely Tom would want to do the same?

'He was genuinely worried that I would be bored and unfulfilled,' reflects Tom. 'Acting was completely other from anything he knew and he just couldn't see that it was a real job.'

In the end Tom politely thanked his father for his concern and promised he'd continue to work hard at his studies. But his mind was firmly made up: he wanted to continue with acting too. It might not work out, but least he could give it his best shot. He'd always have his education to fall back on but if he didn't try, he'd never know.

'We all impose a glass ceiling on our expectations,' he would later admit to the *Daily Mail*. 'I'm an eternal realist and the success rate for being an actor is pretty low.'

In reality, Tom's first taste of success would come much sooner than he could have anticipated. During his first year at Cambridge he was cast in a university production of Tennessee Williams' *A Streetcar Named Desire*. He landed the role of Mitch, played by Karl Malden in the 1951 adaptation headlined by Marlon Brando and Vivien Leigh in the lead as Stanley Kowalski and Blanche DuBois. Mitch was a character going through a mid-life crisis and Tom did his best to replicate the distress and anxiety underpinning his character.

His efforts paid off.

Other cast members in the show were older than Tom

and about to graduate, so a group of agents had been invited to watch the performance. Many of the cast were nervous and desperate to impress the important, influential audience. Tom wanted to do his best to help support his friends and put on a good show. Never did he imagine that one of the agents would walk away with his name in mind.

Lorraine Hamilton, from the agency Hamilton Hodell, had a good reputation for signing Cambridge talent. She already represented Hugh Laurie, Emma Thompson and Tilda Swinton. Tom quickly caught her attention; she was impressed by his stage presence and his interpretation of Mitch. He clearly stood out from the crowd.

The following week she gave him a call. There was a new ITV production called *The Life & Adventures of Nicholas Nickleby* and she wondered if he'd be interested in auditioning.

Tom was offered the role, playing a 'flunky' of Sir Mulberry Hawk (Dominic West). 'I had five days' work and scenes with Dominic, pre-*Wire* [*The Wire* TV series], and Charles Dance and James D'Arcy and I was in; I was hooked,' he gushed.

'I wonder if I hadn't been spotted in that production, would I have had the courage to be an actor? I don't know,' he would later admit to *Esquire* in June 2016.

It was the beginning of something big, although for now he had no idea how successful he would eventually become. His agent strongly advised him to stay on at Cambridge and finish his studies rather than giving up everything right now for acting. 'She said: "Don't leave Cambridge because it's a very special thing and you'll never get a chance to do it again. So what I'll do is I'll look for work for you during the holidays and you can keep doing what you're doing."

'Inevitably, I never got any work in the holidays, I always got work in term-time, but somehow I managed to swing it,' Tom recalled to *Industrial Insider* in 2014.

Throughout his time at Cambridge he continued to star in various productions. When he wasn't studying, he relaxed by playing the piano, guitar, drums, violin, lute and trumpet. Unfortunately, he had to give up playing rugby in order to fit in his new part-time acting career. He admits he was 'very bad at spinning both plates in the air at the same time'.

To compensate for the amount of time he was spending on acting, Tom became increasingly earnest about his studies and pushed himself ever harder. 'Whenever I wasn't acting, I was rigorously working, partly because I enjoyed it, but certainly my experience of university life wasn't conventional, in any sense. I didn't drink nearly enough, I didn't party nearly enough and I was never there, because I was always off somewhere else making a television film; it was all television, mostly, that I did. And some plays, as well,' he told *Industrial Insider* in 2014.

Eventually, and incredibly, though, he graduated with a double first: 'I managed to swing it, by some twist of fate and accident; I managed to get a first twice. I think it was probably due to some abject terror that I was going to fail because I'd spent so much time acting.'

Now, he decided, it was time to focus greater attention on acting. He was already in a very fortunate position: 'Lots of people at Cambridge were really talented, brilliant actors, and they were scrabbling around to get an agent and to enter the business in some way. I already had that very essential thing; somebody who could put me up for work and try and sell me to casting directors and give me a leg-up.'

After giving it some thought, he concluded his best move would be to apply for a place at RADA (The Royal Academy of Dramatic Art) in London. At the time he was already working with Albert Finney and Vanessa Redgrave on *The Gathering Storm*, a TV movie (2002), and so he asked the two seasoned professionals for their advice.

'You know, you're doing tremendously and you're very instinctive and that's the thing that keeps you safe as an actor,' Redgrave told him. But Finney warned: 'Well, the thing is, there's no repertory theatre anymore, which is really where I learnt how to act.'

In the sixties and seventies actors had built the foundation for their careers in the rep theatre. Every week they'd perform a different play, rehearsing during the day and learning to quickly read scripts and build characters. 'Now I don't want to bemoan the loss of it – lots of actors do – but he [Albert Finney] said there isn't this rep system anymore, so drama school really is the only replacement for that experience, where you're free to fail, in a sense and you're free to try new things and play parts you wouldn't necessarily be given.

'Lots of people said, "You're 21 and you've got a great agent, you've got momentum, you shouldn't do it" and I thought, "I want to be an actor for the rest of my life, what's three years?"' he told *Industrial Insider* in 2014.

And so Tom won himself a place at RADA, where he would hone his talents for the next three years. He found himself in the same year as the 'chameleon-like' Andrea Riseborough, two years below the 'prodigious and electrifying' Ben Whishaw and two years above Gemma Arterton, later to get her breakthrough in the Bond movie, *Quantum of Solace* (2008).

'I had an amazing year group; really, truly amazing,' recalled Tom.

At the time, none of the budding actors had been declared a star but it was very obvious they all shared a great talent. 'We're all just young people, messing around and trying stuff out, and that's an enormously stimulating environment to be in. You can see everybody's talent and you get behind them and you know when they're good,' Tom told *Industrial Insider* in 2014.

Meanwhile his agent continued to put him forward for various acting jobs, which helped pay for his studies.

'I loved it,' said Tom of his time spent at the famous drama school. 'RADA is just up by Goodge Street station and I used to run down to the Curzon Soho and the Odeon. I saw everything that came out. And I wanted to be part of it.

'There are still parts of filmmaking that seem very remote.

I've always loved the European tradition of filmmaking. It's something I'll have to work a lot harder on. I'd love to learn another language and be in a foreign film.'

After leaving RADA in 2005, he felt confident he might actually be able to make a living from a profession he truly loved. Only two weeks after graduating he received a phone call that would propel his career forward.

'It was so strange. I was two weeks out of RADA. When you leave, there's a strange period when you're trying to work out how to handle auditions. It was a heatwave and I was watching the Italian film *The Consequences of Love* at the Curzon Soho and got this text from my agent which said, "Call me right now, where are you?" He told me, "You've got to be at BAFTA in 20 minutes",' Tom told *Time Out*.

The call was an invitation to audition for a new independent film called *Unrelated*, directed by Joanna Hogg.

'I was wearing flip flops, shorts and a T-shirt, and said I couldn't go in this gear. She said, "Just apologise for looking scruffy." Little did I know I'd dressed in character. I was disarmed and quite open in that first meeting.'

But his attire was spot-on; he was exactly what Joanna Hogg was looking for.

'I think I'm put off when actors come in who've rehearsed something and it's all very slick,' Hogg told *Time Out*.

The film follows the story of Anna (played by Kathryn Worth), who goes on holiday with her old school friend

Verena (Mary Roscoe) and her family to stay in a rented villa in Tuscany. Following an argument Anna leaves her husband, Alex, at home, but tells Verena he couldn't come due to work commitments. As the holiday progresses Anna snubs her contemporaries to hang out with the younger generation of teenagers in the family group, including Verena's nephew Oakley (played by Tom Hiddleston).

In a bid to forget about her relationship problems, Anna lets loose with the teens, smoking cannabis and even getting involved in a drunken car accident. She promises not to say anything to the adults, but after she invites Oakley to spend the night with her and he turns her down, she goes back on her word. A huge fight ensues and, rejected by the teenagers, Anna is forced to check into a hotel. She later reconciles with her friend Verena and reveals she is unable to have children.

'*Unrelated* was my first job, just two weeks out of drama school, and Joanna [Hogg] and I were as surprised as anyone when the film was taken up and championed by critics and audiences alike, and Joanna was hailed as a new, astonishingly confident, British auteur,' wrote Tom in a diary article for the *Financial Times*.

'I played Oakley, an arrogant, irresponsible, sexually cavalier 19-year-old, and both learned invaluable lessons about the craft of screen acting, and won some stripes on my lapel to be proud of.

'I felt quickly like I understood the character of Oakley in *Unrelated*. I'd never been him. At 19, I was not an alpha male. But I knew those people. I knew his demons and his confidence. I also understood families who had been dysfunctional but were becoming a new unit, with new members.'

During the course of the film Tom and his director Joanna Hogg forged a strong friendship and even after filming wrapped, they stayed in touch.

'Joanna and I stayed in touch a lot, personally,' Tom told *View London*. 'We became very close over the making of *Unrelated* and we've kind of found that we both share quite a reflective, philosophical inclination, as in, quite a lot of times, we're often asking ourselves of identity, self-definition. We're both people who are putting out different products which do provoke people to make assumptions about who we are – Joanna as a director, myself as an actor.'

Indeed Hogg's methods of filming were very different to anything he had experienced before, or would do again: 'She shoots in sequence, which I've never done before or since. And there's a huge freedom to that, because you really do feel like you're living through the journey of the story.

'In another story, because of the way the shooting schedule is organised, it might be that you have to do the reconciliation scene before the argument scene and so quite often there's just a lot of plotting, as an actor, one has to do, like, "So how am I going to be responding to what's just happened?" But that's the craft of acting. And another thing is that there's no costume department or hair and make-up department. So there's no vanity department, basically, which is quite freeing.

'Quite often, Joanna wants to present something that isn't smooth, that isn't polished and is closer to real life – nothing has a cinematic sheen on it.

'And the third thing is that there's a lot of improvisation and there's no formal script. She writes it as a sort of novella and a tone poem, so you know exactly what the jigsaw puzzle's going to look like, but in terms of what's on each piece of that puzzle, it's really very freeing.'

The director in turn was equally impressed. 'Tom can totally transform himself into another human being,' she told the *Telegraph*. 'Stretching himself in new directions and surprising [us] each time. It would be fun to cast him in a musical. I'd like to do that; he has an exceptional sense of rhythm and moves like a dream.'

Hogg's advice would prove fundamental in giving Tom the courage and confidence to sculpt himself a career as an actor. She truly believed he was capable of great things.

'Joanna was actually the first person who said, "it's very easy to place you in a conventional framework as an actor, a young actor. You're going to get offered a lot of period stuff, just because of how you look and how you sound and your education but maybe a more interesting angle would be a contemporary thing, like, despite how you look and sound, you're quite a contemporary soul. So think about that." She gave me huge courage to steer my own boat through the waters of being in this industry,' Tom told *Industrial Insider* in 2014.

Unrelated was released on 19 September 2008 to critical acclaim.

'As if from nowhere, a first-time British filmmaker has appeared with a tremendously accomplished, subtle and supremely confident feature, authorially distinctive and positively dripping with technique,' wrote the *Guardian*.

'*Unrelated* is an emotionally and sometimes wince-inducingly acute debut from British director Joanna Hogg that looks and feels and sounds like few other British films,' said the *Telegraph*. '*Unrelated*, in its understated, eye-catching fashion, is as arresting as any British debut feature since Lynne Ramsay's *Ratcatcher* and Jonathan Glazer's *Sexy Beast*.'

* * *

Despite the accolades heaped on Joanna Hogg, Tom was not instantly recognised as a star. Several rejections for film roles followed. Although disappointed, he was not deterred. While his film career was getting off to a slow start, he was doing exceptionally well in the theatre – a realm that had always been his natural home.

In 2007, he played Cloten and Posthumus Leonatus in Cheek by Jowl's 2007 production of *Cymbeline*, a role that would lead to great critical acclaim. However, he did have a few mishaps along the way.

Every actor experiences a mixture of adrenaline and fear

on opening nights and Tom Hiddleston was no different. He knew the script inside out but first night nerves are always hard to dispel. Unfortunately, there were a few minor hiccups. In the first act, part of the stage furniture was a prop bottle of champagne, which was supposed to stay fixed to a table. When he arrived on stage, Tom accidentally bumped past the furniture and sent the bottle toppling over. Ginger beer spilled all over the floor, creating a sticky mess. For the remainder of the act, actors were trying to dodge a big puddle and not slip on the liquid. Luckily, everyone carried on like the true professionals they were and the audience barely noticed.

The mishap certainly didn't deter critics from singing Hiddleston's praises. In 2007, the *Guardian* wrote: 'Remember that name. One day that lad is going to be a star, and deservedly so.' In fact, his performance was so well received he was even awarded the Olivier Award for Best Newcomer in 2008. Tom was over the moon when he heard the news: at last he was starting to get some recognition, and his career was beginning to take shape.

Even James Hiddleston was forced to admit his son might have a future as a successful actor.

CHAPTER FOUR

'MY HIDDLESTON YEAR'

Most serious actors will attempt to master Shakespeare at least once in their careers. Tom avidly read the Bard's plays and appeared in numerous productions but one in particular would change his life forever.

In 2008, director Michael Grandage cast him as Cassio in an adaptation of *Othello* at the Donmar Warehouse in Covent Garden, London. He would be joining an illustrious line-up, including Ewan McGregor. Taking the preparation for his role extremely seriously, Tom read the script over and over again. He scoured it for details that might shed light on his character; he examined every word of dialogues and mulled over events. He fully immersed himself in his character, trying to imagine exactly what that person might be like.

'When I played Cassio in *Othello*, I imagined what it

would be like to be a lieutenant in the Venetian navy in 1604,' he wrote in a short article for the *Guardian*. He recalled sitting down with Ewan McGregor (Iago) and Chiwetel Ejiofor (Othello) and together they decided that their characters all had 'soldiery in their bones'.

'I took from the script that Cassio was talented and ambitious, with no emotional or physical guard – and that's how I played the part,' Hiddleston explained.

He shared a dressing room with Ewan McGregor, and every night before a performance, Tom would pace the room, trying to imagine himself into the character and 'not get in the way of myself': 'In act two of *Othello*, when Cassio is manipulated to fight Roderigo and loses his rank, some nights I would burst into tears; other nights I wouldn't but I would still feel the same emotion, night after night.'

Tom took to the role easily – he was a natural at reading Shakespeare. In the run-up to the first night the usual emotions of exhilarated excitement, panic and fear consumed the actors. Indeed he was so focused on nailing his performance that he barely noticed a famous face in the dimly lit auditorium during the dress rehearsal. A few rows back, hidden in the shadows, was Kenneth Branagh.

A Shakespearean stalwart, the famous actor and director quickly identified Tom's talents. He was impressed by the rising star's delivery and his natural presence on stage. Once the show was over, he requested an introduction. It was the beginning of a relationship that would put Hiddleston on the fast track to success.

'It was one of the happiest times in my life,' says Tom retrospectively.

Aware he had found a star in the making, Branagh quickly cast Tom as the character Christian in a Radio 3 production of *Cyrano de Bergerac* (2008). The following year, he invited his new friend to play his sidekick, Magnus Martinsson, in six episodes of the BBC1 detective series *Wallander*.

The series was an English adaptation of the Swedish Nordic noir novelist Henning Mankell's Kurt Wallander novels. Kenneth Branagh was to star in the lead role as the eponymous police inspector in the small town of Ystad, Sweden. Branagh described his character as 'an existentialist who is questioning what life is about and why he does what he does every day, and for whom acts of violence never become normal. There is a level of empathy with the victims of crime that is almost impossible to contain, and one of the prices he pays for that sort of empathy is a personal life that is a kind of wasteland.'

The series was touted as a much darker version of *Inspector Morse*.

Filming took place in southern Sweden, and long shoots gave the two actors ample opportunity to forge a solid friendship. On many occasions they would be shooting scenes until the early hours. Both men were extremely well read and would spend hours discussing different authors and plays. They quickly became accustomed to each other's quirks and idiosyncrasies.

During a later interview with *GQ* magazine, Tom jokingly

gave a very astute impression of his friend and mentor requesting breakfast dishes in his trademark plummy tones tinged with a Belfast brogue: 'Well, should one find oneself in the fortunate position of having a choice, for what might be construed as a petit déjeuner, as the French call it, one might possibly prefer, if the hour of the day should demand, to start with a cup of coffee, perhaps a bowl of strawberries and raspberries and, if one was in the fortunate position of requesting a second course, that second course might involve a preparation of eggs, cooked to the inclination of the... and so it goes on.'

Tom admired his friend's ability to spontaneously talk at length about any subject: 'He's got the gift of the gab. I think it's an Irish thing. It comes from some Irish love of words. And then he'll throw in some extraordinary obscenity which will make you laugh!'

During filming he had learned a great deal from his mentor. 'Ken is magnificent,' he gushed. 'I've learnt from his approach to acting, who he is and how he is on set, the questions he asks, the, almost – the restlessness of his mind, in terms of searching out the truth of each moment.

'On *Wallander* he was constantly saying, "I think if I say it as written in the script, it just sounds like I'm in a generic police series. I think in life, this is what happens; I think, Tom, you should take that line, or you should ask me that question, and then I can come up with the answer."'

Although the subject of the programme was dark and gloomy, the cast had exceptional fun off-camera. 'On screen, we try to show what it costs the police, emotionally, to deal with murder victims,' Tom told the *Evening Standard* in 2010. 'But behind the scenes, we're filming in Sweden on Midsummer's Eve, which is like their New Year's Eve, and everyone in the crew is in high spirits. They're so kind and have what I now understand as a Scandinavian sense of humour, very dry and with far fewer taboos than we have.'

But Hiddleston's friendship with Kenneth Branagh wasn't the only relationship to blossom during filming for *Wallander*. His co-star, actress Susannah Fielding, was spotted spending a great deal of time with Tom. The attractive young actress, born and raised in Hampshire, had already featured in an edition of lads' mag *FHM*, so it was perhaps no surprise when the tabloid press started linking the two stars together. Some reports even suggested the pair might be married, although Tom was quick to dismiss the idea as complete nonsense.

'I am definitively not married,' he would later tell reporters. 'That was a big mistake I don't know where it came from.'

Tom is an extremely private person and he didn't like the idea of reporters intruding into his private life. He felt extremely protective of his friends and family and didn't want them to be harmed or disturbed in any way. But the truth was Tom Hiddleston was starting to attract greater public attention because the *Wallander* TV series was well received by critics. In *The Times* Paul Hoggart described Branagh's performance as 'understated, ruminative, warm, sensitive and depressed' and wrote positively of the design and cinematography and concluded that '*Wallander* is that rare treasure: a popular form used for intelligent, thoughtful, classy drama and superbly shot.'

Meanwhile Andrew Billen of *The Times* wrote, 'This distinctly superior cop show is both spare and suggestive, and brilliantly acted.'

The show also had an impact on the tourism industry in Ystad. 'A lot of travel organisers from the UK call and want to include Ystad in what they can offer their clients,' said Marie Holmström, tourism coordinator with Ystad tourism agency. 'This year we had 30% more hotel bookings from Great Britain, compared to last year. Kenneth Branagh says many good things about this town and we have received many requests from the British press.'

* * *

Once filming for *Wallander* was over, Tom landed the role of Doctor Eugene Lvov in Chekhov's *Ivanov* at the Donmar Warehouse. And once again he would be starring alongside Kenneth Branagh, who was to play Ivanov.

'Suddenly we were staring down the barrel of spending an entire year together,' laughed Tom. 'I remember seeing him at a costume fitting and he said, "I'm calling this my Hiddleston year!"'

Once again, Tom fully embraced his character. Lvov was described as 'a prig and a bigot... uprightness in boots... tiresome... completely sincere'. His emotions were locked away... I practised speaking gravely without emotion and

I actually noticed how that carried over into my personal life. I felt a real need to release myself from the shackles of that character,' he wrote in the *Guardian*.

'It's exhilarating to act out the emotions of a character – it's a bit like being a child again. You flex the same muscles that you did when you pretended to be a cowboy or a policeman: acting is a grown-up version of that with more subtlety and detail. You're responding with real emotions to imaginary situations.'

Tom confessed that whenever he appeared in a production, there wasn't a single day when he didn't laugh, cry or scream. 'There are times when I wake up stiff from emotional exhaustion!' he claimed.

At this point in his career, he had to stand back and look at just how far he'd come. His schedule had been extremely packed and the last twelve months had whizzed past, leaving him in a daze. There had barely been time to take stock of the situation. Up until now he had been satisfied with the progress he was making but he had to admit there were greater accomplishments to be made. He had big ambitions and he knew he was capable of achieving so much more.

His family had always been supportive and Diana would forever be telling her son not to be so self-critical but hard-working James Hiddleston had instilled a strong work ethic. It was simply in Tom's nature to always want to do better; commitment and determination being part of his DNA. Besides, it was somewhat galling to watch some of his contemporaries zoom to success so quickly. Of course, he was pleased for them and wouldn't begrudge anyone else's good fortune but it still nagged at him, pushing him to strive harder for greater recognition.

'I'd been acting for about four years and I'd already seen some of my contemporaries rocketing to immediate and extraordinary levels of success,' he told the *Daily Mail* in 2012. 'Gemma Arterton, who was two years below me at RADA, was suddenly the great hope of British acting while I was still grinding away in the theatre. Eddie Redmayne, who I was at school with, was off making movies with Angelina Jolie and Matt Damon. I thought that if it hasn't happened for me, maybe it never will.'

He also recalled nights spent sitting in cinemas, wishing he could break into Hollywood. One dark evening in Malmö, Sweden, during a break in filming *Wallander*, he visited the cinema on a rare night off. *Iron Man* was showing, and Tom recalls being impressed by Robert Downey Jr's return-to-form performance. In his heart, he knew he should be landing similar roles.

In reality, he was already on his way to achieving his dreams. That realisation slowly dawned on him. 'It was only really the experience of doing *Othello* at the Donmar in London and sharing a dressing room with Ewan McGregor, then working with Kenneth Branagh on *Wallander* that made me go, "Hang on, I'd better redraw the map,"' he told the *Express* in 2012. He'd come much further than he'd thought. Success was already well within his grasp.

His next project would involve working with another old friend, this time Joanna Hogg. The pioneering filmmaker invited Hiddleston to star in her next film, *Archipelago* (2010).

'In *Archipelago*, I play Edward, a 28-year-old who has just left a burgeoning career in an investment bank, and has committed to the beginning of his own personal odyssey: 11 months of voluntary service with Aids-suffering communities in Uganda,' Tom told the *Financial Times*. 'His mother and sister have organised a family trip to Tresco, 25 miles off the coast of Cornwall, as a send-off. They are all hoping his father will come down to the island later on, but he never materialises.

'As you may have guessed, the tensions created by his struggle for personal freedom and self-definition, outside of the family unit, are crushing and suffocating. In order to define himself, Edward needs to travel, to journey, to adventure, to set sail, in order to be able to come back, to come home.'

And he couldn't wait to start working with the British director again, adding: 'Joanna Hogg is unique, because she makes films about the people she knows – the English upper-middle-classes – and in a manner inspired by the film-makers she loves – Éric Rohmer, Michael Haneke, and Yasujirô Ozu. I don't know anyone like her. She makes very European films about very British people. Her work is unashamedly austere, challenging, and open-ended. The camera is still, the takes are long, the pace is slow.

'Her characters are quiet, passive, often remote. Nothing much happens, nothing much is resolved. But beneath the surface is a quiet desperation, an undercurrent of a powerful subtext begging to be articulated.'

During filming, Hogg encouraged Hiddleston to improvise and play with his character: 'I just want you to pull out the most vulnerable part of yourself and that's what I want to shoot. I'm not interested in your strength,' she told him.

In truth, she had been mulling over the concept for some time. She'd been toying with the idea of making a film about a young man struggling with his family and his own guilt despite being a good person deep down and so she rang Tom for some background information on what it was really like to be a 28-year-old man.

'Joanna asked direct questions,' he told *Time Out* in 2012. 'What keeps you up at night? What nags at the corners of your soul in darker moments? And the answers were about a struggle to be free, to define myself. That fed into Edward's desire to do something different, something his family found ridiculous, laughable, objectionable, which is this volunteer service in Africa. I've always known what I wanted to do. But Edward doesn't.'

Bizarrely, the actors were actually staying in the same house where filming was done.

'As an actor it's intense,' Tom told *Time Out*. 'If a scene with an argument plays out in the living room, the crew packs up and leaves, and we're still living in that same house.'

It was to prove a very intense experience. In *Unrelated*, Tom had done something similar; he'd shared a room with two of the other teenagers: 'Immediately there's a chemistry because you wake up and go to sleep together,' he admitted.

Before Joanna Hogg had even written her story, she knew she wanted Tom Hiddleston to be involved. Already fleshing out an outline for Edward, she asked avid reader Tom to pick up a copy of Fyodor Dostoevsky's classic work *The Idiot*. In return, he suggested another book that might help inform her sense of the character – but it wasn't in the same literary calibre.

'It was *The Snowman*!' Tom revealed to *Time Out*. 'I don't know how I came to think of it. I think I'd watched it recently and Edward was swimming around in my head. It's beautiful.'

Joanna agreed it was spot-on: 'I saw this boy and thought: Edward is this boy grown up. So those pyjamas Edward wears are those pyjamas from "The Snowman". I don't wear those pyjamas! It helped when we went around getting costumes from charity shops in West London.'

Unlike other big-budget productions, independent producer Hogg didn't set aside much money for costumes. Instead her actors needed to pull together bits and pieces; ultimately, they had to rely on their delivery rather than the outfits they were wearing.

'It's a good way of getting your arms around a project,' Tom explained to *Time Out*. 'It's wonderful when you have a huge costume budget and someone tailors your clothes to your exact measurements. But it depends on your level of vanity, whether you worry about how you're going to look. I respect actors who are true to the character rather than themselves.'

Hogg in turn appreciated his input in the development of her film. 'Tom has become as much a creative collaborator as an actor in the films,' she said. 'We sit around and talk a lot, and these very personal conversations have a way of filtering through to the film itself. The thing with Tom is he's able to make you believe in himself. He has this great transformative skill, but he's also putting a lot of himself into every character, and it gives the performance a whole extra layer. Other actors are just interpreting.'

Their efforts paid off and the film was another success; quite remarkable for a production shot on such a tight budget. Writing in the *Guardian*, Philip French described it as one of the 'three most formally interesting British movies of the past few years'.

'No-one is making movies quite like this beauti-fully composed portrait of a middle-class family,' said the *Telegraph*, rating it four stars.

Alas, Tom didn't have much time to ruminate on the impressive reviews. He was already well underway with his next project. After finishing *Archipelago*, he had literally a week to pack up his belongings. He was selling his flat in Kentish Town, Northwest London, and shifting to sunnier climes, where new adventures and challenges awaited him.

CHAPTER FIVE

THOR

It was a typically sunny day in Los Angeles when Tom received a call from his friend and mentor Kenneth Branagh, inviting him to lunch. It was 2009 – a year after the pair had starred together in *Wallander* and the West End production of Chekhov's four-act drama *Ivanov*.

Now good friends, they had a lot to catch up on. Tom looked forward to sharing some intelligent conversation and hearing about Branagh's latest endeavours. The knighted actor had really taken him under his wing, and even considered the accomplished young man to be his protégé.

'We really clicked,' Tom told the *Daily Mail* in 2012, recalling their time spent on and offstage during the run of *Ivanov*. 'The two characters we played were locked in an ideological battle of wits. It was like old bull, young bull, and we just went at it every night for 95 shows.'

Hiddleston had arrived in LA after being signed by an agent on the back of his performance in *Othello*.

'Come to LA and we'll introduce you to the city,' they told him.

'I auditioned for everything under the sun: television series, films that you've seen, films that have been huge hits – and films that haven't,' he recalled of that time. So far he'd not had much success in making it Stateside but all that was about to change.

Tom knew Kenneth Branagh had come to LA to work on his next project, an ambitious new film based on the Marvel Comics character Thor, produced by Marvel Studios. 'Ken found out he'd got the job in late 2008, when we were appearing at the Donmar together, knocking eight bells of ideological crap out of each other every night in Chekhov's *Ivanov*,' Tom told the *Guardian* a year later.

'Dressed as the self-righteous 19th-century Doctor Lvov, with wire-rimmed spectacles, a pocket watch, grey trousers, a linen jacket and a goatee, I ran up to Ken's dressing room holding a massive empty water cooler that I pretended was Thor's hammer. He looked at me and said, "Don't joke, love, you never know."'

Those words were now ringing true. He was stunned when Branagh invited him to audition for the lead role of Thor. But he was relieved that he didn't have to prove his worth to his old friend. He was fast discovering that Hollywood could be a tough place, but at least Branagh knew he could act. Still, he'd have to do some work to persuade studio bosses.

'Studio executives get nervous about casting new people because the budgets are so big,' Tom admitted: 'No amount of throwing the kitchen sink at them in every audition will ever convince them. You need advocates.'

After discussion with agents, he was told he'd need to bulk up to be in with a chance of landing the part. At the moment his slight physique didn't quite match the look they were after – this was, after all, the God of Thunder.

'I looked at the comics and this guy's huge; he's a man mountain and I wasn't sure that I had it in me to get, to do that, really,' confessed Tom to *Industrial Scripts*. 'I spoke to Ken and he said it wouldn't be a bad idea. So then I spoke to the casting director and they said "just aim for Brad Pitt in *Fight Club*, then." And I was like "oh, just Brad Pitt in *Fight Club*; that will be easy".'

Eager to fulfil this request, Tom set to work. Having played rugby for many years in his youth, he wasn't shy of physical exercise. He increased his running regime, clocking up an increasing number of kilometres by the day, and switched to a more protein-heavy diet, eating 'nothing but chicken' and lifting weights until he 'could barely walk'. Within six weeks he had managed to put on twenty pounds of muscle, bringing his weight to fourteen stone.

'For the very first time in my life I found a personal trainer and was just in the gym for three hours a day, for six weeks, eating five meals a day. I managed to get from 12 stone to 14 and a half stone, and I will probably never look like that again,' he told *Industrial Scripts*.

His family could barely believe the transformation: slim-line Tom now resembled exactly the sort of superhero you'd expect to find in the pages of a comic book.

When studio executives saw his audition tape, they were impressed.

Tom recalls their response: 'They said, "Who is that guy? Why haven't we heard of him before?"' He was then included in the whittled-down shortlist of contenders.

'Every English-speaking actor over six foot was being seen for the part,' he told the *Guardian* in 2011. 'I got down to the final five, which also included Chris's younger brother Liam Hemsworth, Alexander Skarsgård, Charlie Hunnam and another Swedish actor.'

Despite Hiddleston's high-calibre performance and supreme attempts to get into role, he narrowly missed out on the lead. Instead the Australian actor Chris Hemsworth was to play the character of Thor. It seemed the directors were nervous about casting a relative unknown as the headline lead; they needed a big name that would instantly draw an audience to the box office.

'I was waiting to hear whether I'd got the job of Thor or not, but they called Chris on a Wednesday and they called me on a Thursday,' Tom told the *Huffington Post* in 2014. Indeed producer Kevin Feige called Hiddleston personally to let him know he hadn't got the part.

But Tom understood the reasoning. 'Chris Hemsworth is

made out of genetically modified material,' he later joked in a TV interview. 'He's a genetic anomaly! He wouldn't mind me saying that.'

Besides, he couldn't be too disappointed. Although the casting team didn't believe he was the right person to play Thor, they still wanted him to be involved in the project. So they got in touch to offer him the supporting role of Loki, the scheming adopted brother – by no means a consolation prize.

Kenneth Branagh invited Tom for a breakfast meeting.

'Ken told me that every actor has something for free. Jack Nicholson has an irreverence for free, Anthony Hopkins has a majesty and gravitas for free. Idris Elba, who plays Heimdall in *Thor*, has a watchful gravitas for free. He explained that what I have for free is that I can't turn off my intelligence. Therefore Loki would be much more up my street,' he told the *Guardian* in 2011.

'Actually, this is the role that I would want to play,' Branagh admitted in all genuineness to his friend.

More than anything, Tom was relieved the lengthy audition process had come to an end: 'I was just about ready to scream and dance,' he told *Industrial Scripts* describing the moment the call came through. 'It was the longest audition process I've ever been through.'

There had been three auditions in total, over the course of four months. 'My first audition was in January, my second one was in early March and my screen test was in mid-March and I finally got the phone call at the end of April.'

'In a way, it was a gift,' he says, looking back. 'I have no regrets about it at all. I've never once thought, "I wish I were playing Thor".'

Perhaps there was some fractional disappointment, but he admitted his fellow actor Chris Hemsworth was able to portray the character of Thor in a way that he himself could never have done. His physique alone made him perfect for the part.

Much later, on *The Graham Norton Show*, Branagh revealed: 'He gave a brilliant pitch for the part. He wowed the room as Loki and as Thor. We were an emerging and evolving script so it was always changing. But fair play to Tom, he just went for it.'

In turn Tom realised this was a landmark in his career. He told the *Guardian* in 2011: 'I remember shooting the first series of *Wallander* and on my day off I got the train to Malmö and went to see *Iron Man* with Robert Downey Jr. And I came out thinking, "That's so fucking good. But I'm never, in a million years, going to be in a film like that." But then I tested for the part of Loki in *Thor* and came away thinking, "You know, I've got a real chance at this." It was like a light going on. We all impose limits on ourselves. We think, "There's the ceiling and that's as far as I can go." Then something happens and it changes everything.'

Knowing he'd be in LA for some time, Tom rented an apartment.

'I moved into an architect's studio in Venice Beach, California – my home for the six months it took to make

Thor, and I'm unashamed to say they were some of the happiest of my life. I ran along the Pacific Coast every Saturday morning, with the sun on my face, in February, and never for one second took it for granted,' he told the *Financial Times* in 2011.

He was convinced that more than anything else it was his determination and commitment that had earned him the role: 'I learned a lot from that experience,' he admitted. 'Particularly, that if you risk failure, then you also risk success.'

He was also extremely grateful to his friend Kenneth Branagh, who had been instrumental in giving him a helping hand into Hollywood: 'Ken has had a life-changing effect. He was able to say to the executives, "Trust me on this, you can cast Tom and he will deliver." It was massive and it's completely changed the course of what is available to me to do.

'Everybody needs a break. Every actor needs a break. Everyone needs a little bit of belief and I think he believed in me.'

The two men shared a mutual respect. Tom was completely in awe of Branagh's experience and knowledge: 'I've always found him very impressive. He's a person who confounds your expectations — he is not how you expect him to be. He's one of the most industrious, impeccable actors and directors that we have.

'In every possible way, Kenneth Branagh has been my inspiration; there is no way that I would be where I am now without him.'

During preparation for the filming of *Thor*, Tom regularly consulted Branagh for advice on how he should play Loki. After many discussions they shaped the role based on their shared knowledge of Shakespearean plays, giving the comic-book character a further dimension perhaps not instantly obvious to cinema audiences.

'This is going to sound really wanky, but because Kenneth Branagh and I are both such lovers of Shakespeare, we made Loki out of Shakespearean characters,' Tom revealed in an interview with the *Evening Standard* in 2013. 'We talked about *King Lear* with its two brothers, Macbeth with his ambition, the way Iago spins every situation for self-interest.'

He would later describe his complex character to MTV as occupying 'that liminal point between order and chaos'.

Along with reading Shakespeare, Hiddleston also brushed up on his knowledge of comic book heroes after confessing to *Craveonline* that he'd never read any as a child: 'The only thing I had was a game called Top Trumps,' he said. 'I think it's patented by a toy company. It's a really simple game, and you play it with a category of something. So it could be racing cars, it could be motorbikes, it could be fighter planes, and everything is listed according to their vital statistics. Their speed, their acceleration, whatever.

'And I had the Marvel Superhero Top Trumps. So every character had a card, I suppose like a trading card, and all their vital statistics were at the bottom.'

He quickly made up for lost time by collecting as

many comic books as he could get his hands on, telling the *Huffington Post*: 'I read all the comics, all the way back to Jack Kirby and Stan Lee. I also read J. Michael Straczynski's most recent reworking, as well as the Walt Simonson comics. I read the Norse myths, and I listened to Wagner because Loki turns up in the Ring Cycle.'

Tom also kept a scrapbook, saving pictures and descriptions that he believed fitted Loki. He kept it by his bedside just in case he woke up in the middle of the night with an idea: 'I pasted all these pictures and images from the ancient myths and depictions of him in Western art across the centuries. Stan Lee and Jack Kirby drawings, too. So there was always a kind of devilish maniacal agent of chaos that I wanted to get to.'

In addition to the grand efforts put into characterisation, Tom went to great pains to keep his physical fitness in check: 'When we were shooting *Thor*, I'd commute 20 minutes south down the 405 freeway from Venice to the Marvel studio. On Saturdays, I'd run along the beach, along the shimmering Pacific, and I remember thinking: "You know what? This is all right."'

In between running and swimming, he even found time to take up the Brazilian martial art capoeira.

Although he threw himself into his work, he did suffer pangs of homesickness. The bright lights and shallow cynicism of Hollywood felt a million miles from the accepting comfort of the London stage. He missed his friends and family, and longed to visit his mother in

Aldeburgh, where he would often unwind by walking along the seafront, a bag of fish and chips in hand.

After a month into filming *Thor*, he travelled to India, where his older sister Sarah was getting married. She now lived in Chennai with her partner, Yakov Chandy, and the pair hoped to start a family of their own soon. Tom described the experience as 'five days of blindingly bright Indian colour and non-stop Bollywood dancing'.

Regular phone calls home made him feel much better. No matter how challenging the situation might be, he refused to let down his guard. Besides, he wouldn't dream of complaining – especially on set.

Kenneth Branagh found the young actor's approach refreshing. He was very different to the arrogant divas typically associated with Hollywood, parading their swollen egos. Tom was not only extremely talented, he was exceptionally humble, too. But he did notice that, at least initially, his young friend was struggling to adapt.

'[He was] a bit scared and vulnerable, and at times pretty lonely. I think he withstood isolation pangs that might have thrown some people.

'But what I admire about Tom is he's not trying to present the idea that a tortured individual lives alongside this gilded youth. He has a lot of the personal challenges that most people have, but he doesn't look for sympathy by trying to convince people that there's trouble in the kingdom,' he told *Esquire*.

Besides, such emotions were normal. Never once did

Branagh doubt his decision in recommending Tom for the part of Loki. 'Tom sees beyond the surface of things, both as an actor and as a man,' he told friends. 'After excellent work already, I feel sure his best is yet to come.'

Not everything on set went to plan, though.

During one filming sequence, Tom winced with pain when Chris Hemsworth accidentally punched him in the face. The Aussie star had beefed up for the movie and could pack a mean punch. Unfortunately, he misjudged his aim and accidentally made full contact with Tom's cheek.

'You don't make any facial expression when that happens. Just before the blood starts to flow, your face goes incontrovertibly still,' Tom recalled to *GQ* in 2013. 'It looks great in the film.'

And there was another fight scene that would elicit an even odder response from audiences when it was screened. 'I've had some very strange fan mail over the years,' confessed Tom. 'There's a moment in the first Thor movie where Thor and Loki are engaged in a fight. I have a spear in my hand and I make a huge leap to spear Chris – but he dodges out of the way.

'The spear is embedded into the ground, so I use the spear as a lever to spin myself around and kick him in the chest.

'Well, some fans have interpreted this as emblematic of my hidden talent at pole dancing. I've received a surprising number of depictions of myself in a pair of tight briefs and a horny helmet dancing on a pole. That is pretty weird and hilarious!'

Once filming wrapped, both cast and crew knew they had a hit on their hands. And they were right: *Thor* received great reviews, of more below, and the ensuing hype attracted filmgoers worldwide. Remarkably, the film grossed more than £280 million at the box office, paving the way for several sequels.

Just before the release Tom bought a flat in North London and moved back to the UK. He told the *Guardian*: 'It's a wildly exciting time. I've never been in a film that has posters on the tube. And it's not even my face on the poster.'

It was certainly a blockbuster movie, but he hoped his characterisation of Loki had introduced some intellectual depth to the story too.

'There's the action in *Thor*, with big, muscle-bound men smashing things up. There's the humour – my favourite line is when Thor strides into a pet shop and demands a horse. And then there's Loki's psychological depth. I hope it means that *Thor* can appeal to many people on many levels.'

Meanwhile, fantastic reviews flooded in.

'Turn off the snark-o-meter, and this is a return to form for Marvel, introducing a new hero we'll be happy to see again in, oh, about a year or so,' wrote *Empire*.

'What *Thor* lacks in subtlety, it makes up for in bombast – but Kenneth Branagh deserves credit for putting his own personal touch on this superhero epic,' pronounced the *Guardian*.

'With *Thor*, director Kenneth Branagh forsakes Shakespeare to transform the hero of Norse legend into a space-travelling Viking,' noted the *Telegraph*.

But for Tom an even greater result was the change in his father's attitude.

'He's seen that it takes six months to make a *Thor* film. I've described my working process to him; the fact that, some days, I get up at four in the morning and don't get home until nine at night, and he's absolutely acknowledged that that's real work,' he told the *Telegraph*.

Looking back over the past few years, Tom realised just how far he'd come. 'I thought, "I might not do this forever, so I want to have a little walk around the horizon so that I've seen all the little pockets of it,"' he said of his decision to ditch a more conventional career in favour of the stage.

'It was the best thing I could have done. Even though I turned down employment for unemployment, earning money for spending it, and every job I auditioned for I didn't get. All except one. Right at the end, I auditioned for *Thor*. Massive game-changer.'

Embarking on an acting career might have been a gamble, but it had paid off. Along with a more than decent salary, Hiddleston was also receiving recognition on the world stage. He'd well and truly hit the big time.

CHAPTER SIX

THE REAL DEAL

Following the success of *Thor*, Tom's career began to snowball. All of Hollywood wondered where this charming Englishman had come from. He looked fantastic on screen and his acting skills far belied his young years.

Some of the biggest names in film were clambering to work with the charismatic, educated Brit. Stars such as Eddie Redmayne had already proved a hit with audiences and it was obvious cinemagoers had a soft spot for well-spoken actors.

Growing up, Tom had always been a fan of Steven Spielberg, one of the most influential personalities in film. Like many children of the eighties, he'd been weaned on a diet of *Star Wars* and *E.T. the Extra-Terrestrial* so when the hotshot director got in touch, perhaps understandably he was left speechless.

Spielberg was working on a new project, a film adaptation of the popular children's novel *War Horse* by Michael Morpurgo. It had already been turned into an internationally acclaimed production at the National Theatre in London, where puppets represented the horses.

The plot centres round a horse purchased by a Devon farmer and cared for by his son, Albert, who later names him Joey. As soon as World War I breaks out, Joey is sold to British Cavalry officer Captain James Nicholls and sent into battle.

Spielberg had watched *Thor* and was immediately impressed by Hiddleston's performance. He wanted to meet this curious new player on the scene, with a view to casting him in his latest project.

'Towards the end of filming *Thor*, I did a video audition for *War Horse*, and then got a call from my agent saying that Steven Spielberg wanted to meet,' Tom explained to the *Guardian* in 2011. But before their first meeting he was struck numb with nerves. What would he say? How would he act around one of his greatest film heroes? He really didn't want to mess this up.

Even though he'd earned great praise for his portrayal of Loki and had been showered with compliments, Tom was still extremely self-critical and self-doubting. Of course many other rising stars would have been consumed by over-inflated arrogance but Hiddleston has always been a very humble person. It has never been in his character to boast. Every day he'd wonder if all this was really happening: one false move and perhaps his dreams might shatter forever? Would fickle Hollywood wake up tomorrow and turn its attention to someone else? Those questions were constantly racing around his head.

'I was telling myself: "You're about to meet one of your all-time heroes,"' Tom told the *Daily Mail* in 2012, describing the rollercoaster of emotions he was experiencing in the lead-up to meeting his childhood hero. 'I remember going home that night and thinking: "What is happening to my life? How did I get here? I'm about to meet one of my heroes!"

'His films are the reason you're an actor – *E.T.*, *Jaws*, *Indiana Jones*, *Schindler's List*, *Saving Private Ryan*.'

Somehow Tom convinced himself he had to act naturally and just trust his instincts – it would be criminal to do otherwise.

'To thine own self be true,' he reasoned. 'If it's supposed to work out, it'll work out and if it's not, at least you'll know you were yourself.'

* * *

The day of the meeting, Tom was calm and collected. More than anything, he felt a rush of excitement. 'I drove up to his office in Universal City and was shown into a room full of Oscars and a model of the boat he's building as a personal project,' he said in an interview with the *Guardian* in 2011. 'I got talking to his assistant about coffee – it's my vice; Steven avoids it – and how much I love Guinness. She said, "Oh my god, Steven loves Guinness! It's his favourite drink!"

'He walked in at that point and so our first conversation was about Guinness. The ice was broken. He asked about *Thor* because he loves Ken [Branagh], and then we were straight on to Vic Armstrong, who was Harrison Ford's stunt double in all the *Indiana Jones* films and who taught me to ride on *Thor*.'

No sooner had they started talking than the great director was already planning a way to involve Tom in his film. 'And then Spielberg said, "Well, if Vic taught you how to ride, I'd like you to do *War Horse*." I nearly fell off my chair. I was stunned. He offered me the part right there and then! Let me tell you, this never happens. Never. An official offer usually comes in weeks later. I had to ask him to repeat it. At which point I almost burst into tears. Here was the architect of my childhood imagination telling me I'm the real deal.'

He was offered the role of Captain Nicholls, who rides the horse Joey in a cavalry charge at the beginning of the conflict. Tom was stunned; even his agents were speechless. Although everyone had high hopes for him and great faith in his abilities, no one could have predicted this.

'I nearly whooped, wept, laughed and cried,' said Tom, who very soon afterwards began studying his character in depth.

'This is absolutely literal and it's the story of one horse,' he said, describing the plot to *Industrial Scripts* in 2011. 'It starts off in Devon in 1912–14, with a country family, a farming family; father and mother played by Peter Mullan and Emily Watson, son played by Jeremy Irvine. You follow this horse, this horse's trajectory, through the course of the First World War, 1914 to 1918.'

He described Captain Nicholls as 'this agent of separation who divorces the horse from his boy'. But he also identified a softer, nobler side to the army official. After all, despite his actions Captain Nicholls promises he'll return the horse to its rightful owner once the war is over.

'Other writers might have made him quite bluff, disciplinarian and possibly cruel,' said Tom. 'But Michael Morpurgo makes him kindly and decent, upstanding and modest, which I found very moving. That was one of the things that attracted me to the part.'

It was quite a departure from his more recent roles. 'Having dug around in so much damage as Loki, here was a man with such a sensitive soul who found himself in uniform, and fighting on the front line.'

Although his heritage lay in making blockbusters, Steven Spielberg made it very clear he didn't want to make a *Saving Private Ryan* with horses. Instead he wanted to create something 'poetic and romantic'.

'He wanted to retain the magic at the heart of Michael Morpurgo's novel, which is very child-friendly, I suppose,' reflected Tom. 'Of course it's got an epic scope and it's got death and grief and pain in it, but it really is about family and it's above love and he didn't want to make it excessively violent because he wants families to go and see it together.

'I suppose Spielberg's more of a classic storyteller. People say he's too sentimental, but he fully believes in all the themes that run through his work. Family, hope, courage, magic. And on set he's like a 25-year-old. He has this infectious, childlike energy. He cries easily.'

* * *

The movie was mostly shot in the English countryside, in Devon, and other places in southern England resembling northern France. Before filming started, Tom had to brush up on his riding skills.

'We all went on this kind of riding boot camp for about six weeks and I fell in love with horses,' he swooned. As previously mentioned Tom did have some past experience of riding horses, but by his own admission he wasn't great: 'I'd ridden, but badly. And I'd ridden out in L.A. up and down dried-up riverbeds, but I was supposed to be playing a captain of the English cavalry, and some of the stunt trainers thought I looked like a sack of potatoes on a motorbike,' he told *Just Jared* in 2011.

On arrival at Steve Dent's farm, west of London, off the M40, many of his fellow actors had already been practising for a few days. In a diary feature for *Tatler*, Tom wrote that Benedict Cumberbatch (Major Jamie Stewart), Patrick Kennedy (Lieutenant Charlie Waverly) and Jeremy Irvine (Albert Narracott) were already walking with a John Wayne swagger.

'If there is an equestrian equivalent of sea legs, Jeremy had it.'

But the school was already famous for teaching actors horsemanship: 'Civilon, our leading horse Joey, was naturally powerful, noble, quiet and solid as a rock, with glimmering shoulders that boasted a V8 engine – my God that horse can run.

'There's nothing like the feeling of galloping at full speed on the back of a horse. It's like driving fast in a car, but the car is alive. It's a hell of an adrenaline rush,' enthused Tom.

He recalled in his *Tatler* diary having to lead 120 galloping horses at forty miles an hour across four hundred metres of no-man's land during the first day's filming: 'We chase the German soldiers through their own camp and back into the woods behind them and then behind the first line of trees are rows upon rows of machine guns which the British army didn't know were there, and it becomes a kind of coconut shy.'

Fully believing in his actor, Spielberg placed Tom at the front of a charge of 120 stuntmen and he did the scene for real. 'If any of us had fallen off, it would have been incredibly dangerous. Pretty much everything was real except the bullets in the guns. So the German camp had 400 tents and fires and people cooking and extras running around. It just felt like I was there. The adrenaline of going that fast with 120 other horses going that fast behind you and the noise, apart from everything else, I'll never forget the noise of a thousand horses' hooves thundering across the earth.

'It was a massive pinch-me moment,' he recalled. 'As a

child, I used to watch *Indiana Jones* on a loop. For me it was all about Spielberg and Harrison Ford. Then, suddenly, I'm on a horse that I've been taught to ride by Vic Armstrong, who was Ford's stunt double in those films, and Spielberg's calling "Action!"'

Overwhelmed by the experience, he struggled to concentrate. But as the cameras started to roll, he immediately slipped into another world. Every hair on his body stood on end as he spurred his horse onward with the wind rushing through his hair and dust clouds billowing in his wake.

'It was one of the most exciting things I've ever done, not just on film but in my life. Balls out, full throttle, there was no acting required. If any of us had fallen off in that charge we would have been trampled underfoot.'

By the time Spielberg shouted 'Cut!' Tom was bristling with excitement, adrenaline pumping around his body. He'd never done anything like that before: 'I got back to the base camp and Spielberg just literally stuck his head out from behind the tent where the monitors were and stuck his thumb up.

'It's a hard one to beat as an experience and I got to do it ten or 11 times,' he said, still trembling at the memory.

Along with Benedict Cumberbatch and Patrick Kennedy, Tom would ride around, pretending they were in *Indiana Jones*. Indeed doing his own stunts and riding horses for real had a huge impact on his performance: 'We did cavalry charges for real,' he explained to *Industrial Scripts*. 'There's something else that happens when you're doing something physical on-screen; you're just doing the thing, you're not really acting. That's enormously releasing, in a funny way.

'We did all the stunt stuff at the beginning and then we had one scene inside a very, very cosy barracks and suddenly we're like "Oh my God, we've got to do some acting!" because there were no horses to distract us from the machinery of the moviemaking.'

Occasionally the horses could misbehave. Writing in *Tatler*, Tom recalled: 'Sometimes the horses' natural spontaneity comes with complications.'

Civilon, the 'Brad Pitt' of horses 'got bored in one of the quieter scenes and had a gentle nibble of my forearm just when Captain Nicholls was supposed to be biting his lip with a contained sadness and fear.'

Then there was the farting of horses, always at inappropriate moments, which sent the whole crew into fits of laughter.

* * *

Working with Stephen Spielberg was a dream come true for Hiddleston, who called him 'a genius'. He told media later: 'Working with him is one of the greatest pleasures of my life. He's so inclusive and generous. He inspires every person on set to do their best work and that's from stunt directors and horsemasters and his regular crew, actors.'

He came to believe Spielberg had a fondness for British actors too.

'He loves our tradition of performing, he loves our training, he loves our discipline and he kept saying "none of you have any ego, which is wonderful, because you just do it and you're brilliant but there's no, sort of, awful baggage attached to that".'

Getting into character actually proved to be very straightforward for Tom. In preparation he watched several old war films and read a biography of the celebrated English war poet Siegfried Sassoon: 'The First World War was really the war in which Europe lost its innocence. I think up until that point, the British and European life was very natural, very relaxed. I think the First World War and its shocking indifference to human life really made us change the world forever,' he told *Just Jared* in 2011.

He also had plenty of family history he could draw on, and his preparations gave him a good excuse to delve into the past. His maternal grandfather was Vice-Admiral Reginald Servaes, a flag officer commanding the reserve fleet in the British Navy. Meanwhile, his paternal grandfather served in the Royal Artillery. Tom fondly remembers as a child going to the pub with Alexander. Together, they'd sit and eat crisps while watching football and sometimes they would play darts.

It was a very different environment to the world he now inhabited, something he became acutely aware of when he visited his grandfather in 2002 for his ninetieth birthday.

Walking into the pub, he recognised the smell of stale beer in the carpet and the dusty, faded posters peeling from the walls. It instantly took him back to his childhood. In the middle of the room stood his grandfather, surrounded by many other jovial men in their seventies – all speaking loudly with broad Scottish accents. The old men were all part of the same bowls team and loved to share a few jokes over a few more pints of ale.

'Grandad even had his own chair!' says Tom of the elderly relative who was such a loyal regular at the pub he had literally become part of the furniture.

By the time Tom arrived, the men were already very drunk. 'I'd just left Cambridge and had my first proper acting job, making *The Gathering Storm* with Albert Finney,' he recalled to the *Guardian* in 2011. 'It was a complete culture clash. I must have looked like a complete p****.'

Fortunately, everyone was genuinely pleased for Tom and asked lots of questions about his life as an actor. His grandfather beamed with pride. 'Ach, I never thought I'd have a grandson on the telly,' he said, slapping a stunned Tom on the back, before handing him a packet of Mint Imperials and a £5 note.

A military history clearly ran through the family, but it was Tom's great-great uncle who had the most interesting past. Also named Tom Hiddleston, he was a sergeant in the British Army before being killed in action in 1916.

The *Mail on Sunday* printed a faded sepia snap of the soldier to whom Tom bore an uncanny resemblance. 'There's no mistaking the sharp cheekbones, hint of mischief around the smile and the hypnotic eyes,' commented the newspaper.

When the elder Tom Hiddleston voluntarily signed up

for battle, he was just twenty-one and working as a plater (a kind of welder) at Dunlop Bremer and Co. in the local shipyards.

His mother, Rachel, lived in Prospecthill Street in Greenock and was widowed following the death of his father, Alexander, a local shop owner. His unit was the D Battery of the 260th Brigade RFA, part of the 51st Highland Division. In May 1915, they were sent to the defence of Ypres.

During service in the Battle of the Somme he sustained a gunshot wound on 27 August 1916. He was taken back to a British field hospital and doctors hoped he would survive the injury. Sadly, he developed acute cellulites (an infection of the deeper layers of the skin and the underlying tissue) two weeks later and died. It was a common skin infection during World War I and one that claimed many lives.

His mother was devastated when she heard the news, but the entire family was proud of the young man's courage.

His notice of death reads:

DEATHS. On Service. HIDDLESTON – Died from wounds, at No. 6 General Hospital, Rouen, France. Gunner Tom Hiddleston, 1/3rd Highland (Howitzer) Battaliou. R.R.A., younger son of the late Alex Hiddleston, 9 Prospecthill Street, Greenock.

Today, his name is engraved on a memorial on Broomhill Street, Greenock, dedicated to the men of the town who had fought and perished in the war.

'Tom's division was one of the first to be gassed, so he would sadly have been through a lot before meeting his end,' curator Vincent Gillen from Greenock's McLean Museum and Art Gallery told the *Mail on Sunday*.

At school, young Tom Hiddleston was fascinated by the history of the two World Wars. 'I always found the extraordinary loss of life in the First World War very moving,' he told the *Independent* in 2012. 'I remember learning about it as a very young child, as an eight- or nine-year-old asking my teachers what poppies were for.

'Every year the teachers would suddenly wear these red paper flowers in their lapels, and I would say, "What does that mean?"

'And in history, the next thing you learnt was that there was this terrible, terrible war, from 1914 to 1918, when the country lost an entire generation of young men. And I remember that really affecting me at a very young age.'

At school, Tom enjoyed playing the trumpet and describes it as his 'musical instrument of choice'. He recalls being selected at the age of twelve to play the Last Post on Remembrance Sunday. 'I remember feeling the weight of that,' he said. 'That I was heralding the two minutes' silence.'

It's a memory he holds dear to this day. He had been touched not only by his own family's involvement in the war, but the large-scale suffering experienced by so many others. Their courage should never be forgotten; lessons must be learned from the terrible nature of war, where ultimately no one really wins.

It was a subject Tom felt passionate about and he had devoured many books on the subject, right through childhood and into his adult years. One day, during filming for *War Horse*, he even told his director Steven Spielberg that 'Americans don't really understand' the British attitude to the Great War.

'It was quite a European war until 1917, when the Americans joined up. They don't have the same sense of the loss of innocence and the cataclysmic loss of life. A whole generation was wiped out,' Tom told the *Independent*.

No amount of homework, though, could substitute for great acting skills on the day.

'I learn the lines as soon as I can and then the challenge really, for filming, is to show up and be there and respond to what's around you,' he explained to *ETOnline* in 2013. 'That's where the gold dust is. It's really strange, no amount of preparation will help you with the magic of spontaneity on the day [of filming]. You have to do all the homework to get yourself into the period, the costumes, the style, the voice, the hairdo or whatever it is, but once you've done all that work, you have to kind of let it go and just be there. If you're always thinking about it, it just looks a bit over-thought.'

When *War Horse* was released in 2012, it earned $177.6 million at the box office. Tom was praised for his tear-jerking performance.

'*War Horse* is bold, exquisite family filmmaking in the grandest Hollywood tradition. Be warned: whether you're a hippophile or not, it's a four-hankie moviegoing experience,' said *Empire*'s Ian Freer.

'Steven Spielberg's *War Horse* is a soaring, sprawling epic that harks back to the dream-big visionaries of old Hollywood,' declared the *Telegraph*.

Spielberg himself even likened Hiddleston to a young Errol Flynn.

But he wasn't the only leading director to be enamoured of Tom's acting skills: Woody Allen was also interested in signing the delightful British actor for his latest project. He was about to start work on *Midnight in Paris* (2011) and he thought Tom would be perfect for the role of the American novelist and short-story writer F. Scott Fitzgerald.

Keen to have him involved, Allen folded the script into an envelope and penned a letter saying: 'Dear Tom, here's the script, I'd love you to play the part. We're shooting in Paris in the summer.'

It was a very flattering request, and one that Hiddleston accepted without hesitation. He was stunned at the offer. 'I didn't audition,' he revealed to the *Independent* in 2012 'I didn't even know he was making a film!'

Tom was on set for about three weeks. 'Woody's quite a remote director,' he mused to *Industrial Scripts*. 'He's not particularly hands-on, he's not interested in process, in how individual actors get to where they need to get to. He's shooting, he wants to shoot.'

He recalled scenes where Allen would idly invite the actors into a room and instruct them to 'say something'.

'I'd say, "What, you want me to improvise?"' said Tom. 'And he'd say, "Yeah, yeah – and maybe make it funny."

'But he's fun, he's got a real twinkle in his eye still and I think he was having a good time on this one. It's a love song, or a love letter, to Paris. He shot it beautifully.'

* * *

In 2011, Tom also starred in Terence Davies' adaptation of the Terence Rattigan play, *The Deep Blue Sea*. Amusingly, the film shared a title with the sci-fi horror movie *Deep Blue Sea*, focused on the fallout of a disastrous attempt to genetically engineer sharks.

Tom couldn't resist mentioning it to his director. And in a bizarre twist of fate he would later discover over dinner with his friend Samuel L. Jackson that he'd actually appeared in that movie.

Hiddleston starred as Freddie Page, a World War II soldier forever clinging to his moments of glory during the conflict. While the rest of the world has moved on, Freddie is still stuck in 1940. 'He's suffering from post-traumatic stress; all his friends are dead,' Tom explained to the *Guardian* in 2011 in an analysis of the character.

'And if you survive that experience – the Blitz, the Battle of Britain – then all you want to do is drink and sing. Play golf all day and drive 90mph down the Great Western Road. Freddie has this amazing, superficial vitality, but underneath that is a kind of great spiritual desolation.'

Freddie uses his charisma and charm to seduce lonely

married woman Hester Collyer, played by Rachel Weisz – 'I fought in the Battle of Britain, old fruit,' he tells her in the movie. 'It was childish people like me who saved us from invasion.'

Before shooting began for *The Deep Blue Sea*, the director, Terence Davies, invited the cast to join him for a viewing of the 1948 film *Letter from an Unknown Woman*. Afterwards they all went to the pub, where Davies recited a sonnet and told everyone they were about to make a film about love.

'I mean, that's Terence. He's different from Spielberg,' Hiddleston told the *Guardian*, smiling fondly at the memory.

While auditioning for the role, he watched *Distant Voices, Still Lives*, a 1988 film written and directed by Terence Davies. He enjoyed it so much he was compelled to write an article for *Harper's Bazaar*. 'Though it's always been highlighted as one of the greats from this country, I'd never seen it so I thought this was the moment to do it. And it just knocked me for six,' he gushed.

'I was struck by the confidence that Terence had in his own style; so poetic, so moving, so simple.'

The film follows the story of a working-class family in 1950s Liverpool. 'It's a Britain I felt I recognised because my paternal grandparents were Scottish working-class people from Greenock in Glasgow. My grandfather was a shipbuilder who moved with the industry to live in a bungalow in Sunderland,' he added.

Tom admitted he didn't see his father's parents very often,

but he could easily identify parallels between their lives and those portrayed in the film. 'That sense of what it was like after the war when there was rationing and the country was rebuilding itself, when it was building a National Health Service, and people still sang in the pub. That huge sense of bonhomie after just stamping out fascism in Western Europe. But also captured in the film is that great deal of emotional repression and domestic pain.'

He believed the drama was in fact a reflection of Davies' own past, which had been 'bleached of colour' in a post-war era.

Hiddleston also praised the music. Singalongs down the pub were something Terence Davies had spoken about in great detail when making *The Deep Blue Sea*: 'He talked about the times where it may have been 10 o'clock at night, and if you walked past four or five pubs and in every single one, people would all be singing together,' said Tom.

'I always remember the very beginning of the film,' he added, returning to the subject of *Distant Voices, Still Lives*. 'A soprano sings the words: "there's a man going round taking names" over a shot of an empty staircase before we see the family preparing for their father's funeral. It's hard to describe when a film makes an emotional impact on you, but that poignancy just split me down the middle.'

It appeared Tom had found himself a comfortable niche playing period roles. This was perhaps due to his interest in history and a desire to meticulously explore the past but above all else, he looked and sounded the part: 'When I first left drama school, I walked into meetings, saying "Well, what do you want? I can be whatever you want" and then it took me a while to understand, to just know what I am and to say, "This is what I can bring and I'd love to do it if you do [want me] and if you don't, that's fine,"' he told *Industrial Scripts*.

When asked by the *Guardian* why he was drawn to so many period roles, he replied: 'I don't know. It's possibly something to do with British cinema. If you look at the best and the worst stuff we've produced recently, it's all set in the past – *Tinker, Tailor, The King's Speech*. Somehow the past is a safe place to explore our collective cultural neuroses or whatever it is.

'But it's probably to do with me as well. I wonder if it has something to do with what people perceive as my class or my education or my physique. I suppose I fill a slot.'

During the filming for *Unrelated* in 2006, the director Joanna Hogg, who had since become a good friend, had warned Tom to be wary of being typecast.

'It's going to be very easy to put you in period stuff,' she told him.

'She's right,' concluded Tom, several years later. 'When a casting director sees a Cambridge graduate who's tall, well-spoken, classics degree, they think, "Put him in a waistcoat and send him out,"' he told the *Guardian*.

'But that wasn't the reason I became an actor, to fill that niche. It was because of much more muscular things: *In The Name Of The Father, One Flew Over The Cuckoo's Nest, The French Connection*. It was because of Brando and De Niro. So I've always tried to resist it. I never wanted to be the go-to guy for tails and waistcoats.'

However, he was realistic about how he was currently perceived in the industry. He wasn't really in a position to pick and choose roles just yet: 'It's so funny, the illusion that any of us have any choice. Unless you're Tom Cruise… And I'm not Tom Cruise.'

He might not have reached the A-lister stratosphere just yet, but Tom Hiddleston's star status was fast rising. Yet he made sure he never forgot his roots. A humble person by nature, he hated to brag about his achievements. He made a point of keeping his priorities in check. So when his old college teachers at RADA asked him to come in and give a talk, he made sure he could find the time in his schedule.

'Some of the staff wanted me to come back and give dispatches from the front line, to give an illustration of what students might expect on the other side of their training,' he explained to the *Independent* in 2012. 'I sat in this room where I'd practised sword-fights and sonnets and Stanislavsky and it felt like I was there yesterday. And I remember saying: "I'm supposed to be sitting in the chairs where you are, listening to Mike Leigh or Michael Sheen or whomever." I couldn't believe I was the person giving the talk.'

It had been a crazy, whirlwind year. Tom was hurtling towards the big time, and even if he'd wanted to slam on the brakes, he wouldn't know how.

For now, he'd just have to hold tight and enjoy the ride.

CHAPTER SEVEN

HIGHS, LOWS & HIDDLESTONERS

There was a time when it seemed only American actors would ever be cast in blockbuster movies. The likes of Brad Pitt and Leonardo DiCaprio were classed as A-listers, guaranteed to attract audiences and boost ticket sales in cinema theatres. It was a safe bet to employ actors with a proven track record. But in recent years things had started to change. British actors were now making their way in Hollywood and landing some of the parts previously considered out of their reach. Mainstream audiences were becoming more open-minded, and directors were taking note. In particular, the British accent seemed to appeal to American viewers who'd fallen in love with gentlemanly types such as Hugh Grant.

Tom Hiddleston agreed he was fortunate to be living in a golden age when a young generation of British actors could finally enjoy some success. 'Maybe there was something that happened around the time Hugh Laurie started to be in *House* on TV,' he pondered in an interview with *Time Out* in 2016. 'What trickled down to my generation was a sense that as a British actor you didn't need an invitation to go over to America, you could just go and try your luck. I think that is what's happened.

'British actors who are succeeding – like Tom Hardy, Benedict Cumberbatch, Nicholas Hoult and Idris Elba – these are people who decided to go out there and see what happened. Before then, you had to be in some extraordinary British success and then you could head out there. I remember that new sense of possibility.'

Hiddleston was certainly part of a new vanguard, storming to success in the box office. He was fast becoming a household name and magazines were inviting him to appear in photo shoots. The fact he was also very good-looking no doubt propelled his career that little bit further. He was perfect star material: a pin-up with brains and exceptional acting skills. Directors surely rejoiced in casting an actor not only able to do the job with ease but whose fan base would guarantee sufficient interest in a film.

'A Hamlet among hunks,' declared one American film critic.

His journey to Hollywood might have been slow, but Tom had never considered giving up. Besides, he knew he still had much more to achieve. Every day, he pushed himself further. He craved new projects and loved the variety of work he was now being offered. Not knowing where he might be or what he might be doing in six months' time was exhilarating.

'I enjoy not knowing where the next job is coming from,' he told *Metro*. 'I love opening a new diary on New Year's Day and thinking: "I have no idea what's going to happen this year." I could work in a country I've never been to or learn new skills for a role.'

Indeed the preparation process was one of the elements Tom enjoyed most about his job. It was also a skill and commitment which set him apart from many other actors. As soon as he was briefed about a new role, he'd immediately start researching the background to the character, looking at their personality and the environment they inhabited. He eagerly drew on his knowledge of history, literature and the classics. An avid reader, he had a good foundation to build on.

Once he'd mentally mapped out his new character, he'd get to grips with the physical aspects of the part. How did they walk? How did they look? How did they conduct simple daily activities like eating, drinking and sleeping? All of this made him a rounded actor. Being set new challenges kept his mind active and his passion alive.

'The breadth of experience is where the juice is for me,' he admitted in an interview with *Metro*. 'In the past year I've played the Norse god of mischief, a British cavalry officer in World War I and a fighter pilot. A part of me has experienced all those things. There's something amazing about being able to step into these people's shoes.'

Hiddleston was clearly on a natural high. Success had escalated and he'd barely had a chance to truly appreciate just how significantly his life had changed in the last few years.

'You never get used to it,' he said. 'It's really been amazing and only recently have I been able to have a bit of headspace to sort through the boxes of everything, to process it. It's been more than I'd ever dreamed of.'

But he knew very well that everything could fall apart tomorrow. After all acting was a fickle industry and there were never any guarantees. Only a lucky few could ever make a comfortable living from the profession. Praise from the press could swiftly be followed by criticism and jibes. Tom was no pessimist but he was realistic about what the future might hold. For now, it was just important to take everything in his stride. He was tough enough to deal with whatever challenges might be thrown in his path. Years of rejection and fruitless auditions had equipped him with a thicker skin. He no longer wallowed in self-pity and doubt; he would simply do better next time. Disappointment had been replaced by determination.

'I'm painfully aware of the fragility of things,' he admitted to the *Telegraph* in 2014. 'Because the hard bits are always just around the corner from the easy bits.'

Every day he woke up grateful for the opportunities he'd been given. He never forgot how hard his father had worked to pay for his education, and he couldn't be thankful enough for the introductions his mother had given him to the theatre. He refused to look too far ahead – in fact, the idea of what might happen in the next few years was actually quite a daunting prospect.

'Truly, everything that has happened to me has been beyond any reasonable expectations that I may have had,' he told the *Telegraph* in 2014. 'It all happened so quickly, I'm just concentrating on putting one foot in front of the other.'

For the time being he continued to enjoy a degree of anonymity. Although his name was rolling at the top of the film credits, he could still go for a walk close to his home in North London's Chalk Farm without too many people batting an eyelid. Perhaps, occasionally, someone might ask him for an autograph or selfie, or would ask if he was 'that bloke out of *Wallander*' – but he certainly wasn't being chased down the street or having to travel with a bodyguard.

All that might change one day, friends warned.

'I'm trying to cross every bridge when I come to it. I think it would be very dangerous to start planning the date at which I will be unable to go to Sainsbury's!' he retorted.

Although Tom was determined to remain grounded, his busy career had undoubtedly impacted on his social life. While filming, he would spend hours on set, often in locations far from home. He made an effort to keep in touch with friends and family, but differing time zones – not to mention sheer end-of-day exhaustion – posed great challenges.

Some days, he would film long into the night and all he could think about was the dwindling number of hours' sleep he might get before having to rise early the following morning. The only new people he met tended to be fellow actors, and there was barely any time to forge new relationships – or even to develop existing ones.

For several years Tom managed to keep his romance with actress Susannah Fielding relatively hidden from the press. As mentioned earlier the pair had met during filming for *Wallander* and had been linked on several occasions, with some newspapers even suggesting they were married.

Fiercely private, Tom preferred not to talk about his personal life in interviews and tended to steer away from the subject if ever uncomfortable questions were posed by prying journalists. But they were photographed together at a variety of high-profile public events. In 2011, they were snapped smiling, hugging and kissing at the 36th Annual Toronto Film Festival and premiere of *The Deep Blue Sea*.

On the surface everything seemed to be going well but cracks in their relationship were starting to emerge. The pressure of Tom's increasingly gruelling schedule was beginning to take its toll. As work commitments grew, he had less and less time for Susannah. In the end, they decided it would be best to part ways for good.

Tom never spoke about the break-up publicly, but hinted in interviews that his career had been to blame. 'Acting just demands everything and if you don't give it everything, there will be someone behind you who will,' he told the *Daily Mail*. Although he refused to be pressed for details on specific love interests, he did speak freely about the qualities he looked for in a potential partner. Clearly, the females in his close-knit family had been hugely influential in shaping his view of the perfect woman.

'I like strong women,' he told Irish reporters. 'My mother and sisters are very strong women, immensely independent and very capable and that's what I feel comfortable with. My mother places a huge importance on decency and kindness and always has – and the older I get, the more I realize how rare that is.'

For now, though, he would have to settle for being single.

But it wasn't just his romantic relationships that were being jeopardised as a consequence of his soaring career. Some friendships were also suffering. A real low point came when Tom accidentally missed his best friend's wedding. The almost unforgivable mishap occurred when the actor had been invited to screen test for *War Horse*.

'It was one of those crazy things where I'd said I'd be there – even if Spielberg called,' he recalled. 'And Spielberg did call and I wasn't there.'

When he realised what had happened, he felt extremely ashamed of himself. 'We fell out really badly,' he told the *Mirror*. 'It's OK now. He read me the riot act and then we went out and got slammed.'

Along with healing friendships, Tom also had his own health to consider. He admitted on several occasions to feeling like 'the Walking Dead'.

His friend Joanna Hogg was acutely aware of the perils presented by fame. She'd always feared stardom could in many ways end up hampering the talented young actor's career.

'Sometimes an actor can have too much success,' she told the *Guardian*. 'It's more the fault of the audience than the fault of the actor, but it impairs our sense of them. We start seeing them as an actor as opposed to the character they're playing. I don't know how Tom can avoid that, because he's obviously going to get more and more high-profile.'

Listening to advice from his closest friends, Tom made sure he took time to relax at his North London home. His cat, Bentley, would keep him company, along with his two sisters.

One of his favourite pastimes was to hang out with his young niece.

'I'm called "Uncle Yay Monster" because when we run, she basically wants to run as fast as me but she can't, so after a while I just pick her up and she screams: "Yay!" It's exhausting, but enormous fun.'

At home, he loved to watch episodes of the cult British comedy series *Fawlty Towers*. 'It's really stupid,' he explained to an American journalist from the gossip and entertainment website *Just Jared*. 'It's about a guy played by John Cleese who runs a hotel and he is the grumpiest, most misanthropic man you could ever hope to meet. Why would he run a hotel? Why would you run a hotel if you hate people? People turning up to the hotel is a massive hindrance and a bore for him, so the comedy comes from, of course, the fact that it's an enormously popular hotel.'

Spending time at home between projects allowed him to reflect on his burgeoning career. Stepping away from the madness for a few weeks helped him to maintain some sort of balance. 'You just have to focus on the work and not allow your head to be turned by stuff that doesn't matter,' he concluded to *Industrial Scripts*. 'The work is the only thing you can control. Everything else – how I am perceived by anyone else – I can't control.

'You can't prepare yourself for loss of anonymity until it happens, so there's no question that initially it's confusing. But, I hasten to add, there's nothing more boring than listening to actors whining about fame. It's allowed me to do really interesting work.'

No matter who he was talking to – even journalists – Tom attempted to give genuine and heartfelt responses. He'd always promised to be true to himself.

'I have tried with all of my power for there not to be any inauthenticity,' he once claimed in an interview. 'There is no version of me presented to you that's been created or is artificial. The people I've always respected have an integrity that is unassailable.

'But I won't be the first person to have thought that. I'm only in control of my own integrity. I'm accountable for everything I've done and I understand that. Everything else is out of my control.'

Such honesty and humility were all too rare in the film industry. Directors found Hiddleston's approach refreshing. Not only was he a talented and able actor, he was also a very pleasant and amenable colleague.

'Tom is the consummate gentleman, pleasant to everybody he meets, from royalty down to the lowliest runner on set,' a close friend revealed to the *Daily Mail* in 2016. 'You'll struggle to find anyone with a bad word to say about him. He gives the impression of being supremely relaxed, but make no mistake, he has worked tirelessly to get where he is today. Talent only gets you so far.'

But the same friend also confessed that fame had brought with it inevitable loneliness: 'Being so focused on success isolates him. Hundreds of people consider themselves his friend, but probably no more than half a dozen truly know him – if that. As for women, they are only allowed to get so close, then he moves on. But being a chameleon suits him. It's his shortcut to success. That and a complete lack of fear.'

The latter statement wasn't completely true. Like anyone, Tom suffered his fair share of fear and anxiety. Since childhood, he had always put an enormous pressure on himself to succeed. The idea of unfilled time slipping away from him was his greatest nightmare.

'I have a terrible fear of wasting time,' he revealed to *GQ* in 2016. 'Who knows? Maybe I should relax a bit. Maybe working too hard is wasting time. I have a fear of regret. I'm not afraid of death, although I know that sounds odd.'

There was one other thing that sent shivers up Tom's spine – sharks! Watching the 1975 film *Jaws* as a child had forever marred his opinion of the sea creatures.

'I'm terrified of sharks,' he admitted. 'Nature has designed the ultimate killing machine. I love swimming in the sea and don't think about sharks until I'm the furthest person out from the shoreline and then the John Williams' *Jaws* theme starts in my head.'

Although the circle of close friends surrounding him was small, the number of admirers seeking his attention was rapidly rising. Eager fans started setting up Tumblr sites and social media pages dedicated to the actor. The most dedicated and avid followers referred to themselves as 'Hiddlestoners'.

Tom thought the term was 'quite creative' but found the whole thing to be 'an odd experience'.

'It's a whole other world,' he would later tell chat-show host Graham Norton on his BBC1 show. 'They're mostly very sweet.'

The term would even make its way into the website *urbandictionary.com* and was defined by contributor Ceejay21 as: 'A person in a community that admires Tom Hiddleston':

Hiddlestoners are not part of a cult that worships Tom (like many people think), they are a community that admires him for the many great things he's done; he's a man who's inspired many friendships across the globe. Hiddlestoners admire him by drawing him and his many characters, by talking about him with other fans (whether that's IRL or online) and by writing fan fiction about him and his characters.

The hashtag Hiddlestoner was also trending on Twitter, with loyal users declaring: 'I'm proud to be a #Hiddlestoner'. Fans revelled in Tom's acting skills, the intensity of his voice when reciting poetry, his smile and even the way he licked his lips. In an interview with the star, entertainment and gossip website *Just Jared* told the actor: 'Do you know what happens when they get excited to see you? They get a Hiddleboner.'

Tom was stunned and amused. 'I didn't know that!' he laughed. 'They get a Hiddleboner. That doesn't seem to be related to my name anymore! Hiddleston, yeah, but the boner...

'Hiddlestoner, I can see that, because my name is there.

'OK. Wow. I should be hugely flattered, shouldn't I? I am enormously honoured and flattered.'

Some bemused reporters started referring to the Hiddlestoners as 'fanatics' but Tom would quickly leap to their defence, saying he preferred to call them 'passionate'. When meeting his fans he always made an effort to be polite and accommodating. If selfies were blurred, he'd suggest retaking the picture. Often he used the greeting 'Darling' when speaking to them and was more than happy to freely distribute hugs, all of which made him even more popular.

None of his actions, though, were cynical ploys to boost his popularity. Tom genuinely appreciated the loyalty of his fans, although – humble as ever – he couldn't quite understand why they should be lavishing so much attention on him.

'I get letters from some of the Hiddlestoners, and it's some of the most articulate, eloquent writing I've ever read,' he revealed to website *Bustle*. 'I should be so lucky that I have an army of followers. My goodness!'

CHAPTER EIGHT

SHAKESPEARE'S GLADIATOR

Almost overnight Tom Hiddleston had become an internet sensation. Fans searched tirelessly for news about their favourite star and watched snippets of interviews on YouTube. They analysed his answers on chat shows and swooned over his consistently flawless delivery.

Part of the attraction, commented newspapers and magazines, was his well-to-do background. He fitted neatly into a group of Eton-educated, well-spoken British actors currently storming Hollywood. Eddie Redmayne, Harry Lloyd and Harry Hadden-Paton were all seemingly cut from the same high-quality cloth.

Although Tom fully appreciated why the group of actors was so often lumped together, he vehemently denied his success had anything to do with privilege. 'I'm wary of labels,' he insisted. 'As an actor, the labels that are so easily attachable to me – like Old Etonian or Cambridge graduate or RADA alumnus – are, in a way, the least interesting things about me. I've had to do a lot of work taking off those jackets. The last thing I ever want is to be pigeon-holed,' he told the *Daily Mail* in 2012.

In the early days, when he first started out as an actor, Tom recalled seeing several raised eyebrows during auditions when he revealed that he'd been educated at a 'posh school' – 'I was meeting lots of casting directors and you'd feel the atmosphere change in the room when I said where I went to school. Casting directors would go, "OK, so you went to Eton", and immediately you're put in a box. The whole point of being an actor is you don't want to be put in a box!

'It's true of everyone in this country; we're all so much more than we're allowed to be by this predisposition to keep people in their lane.'

He hated the way people stereotyped students from Eton, assuming they were all toffee-nosed megalomaniacs born with silver spoons in their mouths. 'People think it's just full of braying toffs, who are arrogant and chauvinistic, senseless and ambitious, who are destined to run the country and steal all our money. It isn't true. There are a few people like that but that's one or two in a school of 1,200,' he added.

He believed the focus on his past had a lot to do with Britain's general class neurosis. 'The one thing I despise is how everything artistic, political or intellectual has to be refracted through this prism of class-consciousness. It probably is more sensitive to me but everything becomes really narrow-minded and pedantic and bigoted.'

What difference did it make where he went to school? He'd worked hard all his life to get his breaks. His father had worked even harder to secure him a decent education in the first place. Tom could never forget what James had done for him. Painfully aware of how difficult the journey had been for his family, he felt even more angered by any dismissive assumptions that his career path had been easily paved.

All his life his father had worked hard to give his children the best start in the world. 'So once you've seen that, someone who's come from nothing, trying their hardest to give their child the best education, and then you get out the other side and everyone throws fruit at you,' explained Tom.

As far as he was concerned, his success as an actor had been well earned. Yes, he was fortunate enough to have been given a good education, but no one had handed him his career on a silver platter, he'd worked just as hard as any other actor. The constant stream of comments about the number of middle-class actors in the profession made him feel uncomfortable.

'It's socially divisive in a way it shouldn't be, because I think wherever you are from you should be able to follow your passion. Wherever you went to school, if you have something authentic to contribute, you should be allowed to.

'There is an acknowledged problem of access and inequality of opportunity – I don't know how to remedy that. I'm on everyone's side; I'm on the side of the actors. I'm not there to divide the world into pieces.'

But after much reflection Tom admitted he was becoming much more politically aware as he grew older. He understood why people might complain about unfairness and injustice. It was true – it was easier to get a head start in life if you had money.

'There's a justified anger about inequality of opportunity,' he mused in one interview with the *Telegraph* in 2016. 'People feel that spheres of influence, like politics and the arts, have become the preserve of a privileged few.'

But he thought it was unfair to pick on certain individuals, adding: 'I do think the debate can become unnecessarily prejudicial when individuals are singled out. I've known Eddie [Redmayne] since 14 and I've never seen anyone work so hard!

'But actors who didn't come from privately educated backgrounds, like Julie Walters and David Morrissey, have said, "if I was an actor now, I wouldn't make it." The grants aren't there.'

When Tom attended RADA, a three-year course had cost him £3,300. 'Now it's £30,000!' he exclaimed to reporters. 'That needs to change.

'It is unhealthy for any society to be represented in any sphere of life, including the arts, by one social group. I understand that. I strongly agree with that. More must be done to keep the doors open for everyone. The picture of your life shouldn't have to be dictated by the circumstances in which you were born. Everyone deserves the chance to follow their chosen vocation. Britain is not yet a meritocracy. I hope that changes in my lifetime. If I could think of an easy solution, I'd advocate it right now. These are complex, uneasy times.'

But he refused to apologise for his past. As far as he was concerned he had nothing to hide and he didn't have a bad word to say about his old Etonian stomping ground: 'I've been blessed with an extraordinary education. I feel privileged and I know I've had an enormously pleasant life. But it also has its complexity. I'd love to round out the rosy picture with some shade that would give you some more detail, but it's not my past,' he told the *Evening Standard* in 2013.

For the time being he had to accept people would continue to label him a 'posh boy' actor for some time to come. He could only hope that by taking on a variety of different roles, the public might come to understand the breadth of his talents: 'The reason I've chosen the projects I've chosen is to prove to myself and other people that I'm more than that.

'Perhaps the reason I do what I do is to prove that I'm not who you think I am. And I think part of the pleasure I get from acting is in defying expectations: my own and everyone else's!'

When one journalist asked if he'd like to play a

working-class character on a council estate, he replied enthusiastically: 'I'd love to. It's exciting when you have the chance to do something that isn't your natural inheritance.'

*   *   *

Despite Hiddleston's desire to spread his wings, though, for now his natural home was still in the classics. The call for his next project came in May 2011 while he was packing his bags for a trip to LA. In the background the TV was blaring as he neatly folded his trademark white shirts.

'Prince William was marrying his bride, Kate Middleton, and they were becoming the Duke and Duchess of Cambridge,' he recalled.

Halfway through the televised ceremony, he was interrupted by a phone call: it was the director Sir Richard Eyre. 'Would you like to play Prince Hal in *Henry IV, Part 1* and *Part 2*, which I'm directing for the BBC?' he asked Tom, who later confessed he'd always dreamed of playing the role.

'Prince Hal is just one of those amazing roles in all dramatic literature for a young man,' he told the website *Collider*. 'He undergoes the great classical arc of the wild and indulgent rebel who is testing his limits and stretching his boundaries, and then eventually taking responsibility and becoming the man that he becomes, which is one of the great warrior kings of England. As a story arc, it's basically perfect. I'd always dreamt of playing it… and Richard Eyre is someone that I've respected all my life.'

The director had been in charge of the National Theatre when Tom was a teen, and was responsible for many of the productions that ultimately helped shape Hiddleston's interest in acting. He saw Ian McKellen in Ibsen's *An Enemy of the People*, Vanessa Redgrave and Paul Scofield in *John Gabriel Borkman*, Michael Gambon as Falstaff, and Simon Russell Beale play Hamlet and Iago. 'It's where I really discovered drama,' he claimed. 'I loved movies, but movies were made in America, in my mind. So, my great passion for acting was born out of a lot of theatre going, as a teenager, and under the aegis of Richard Eyre.'

Tom still refers to the moment the great director called as 'amazing'.

'I don't know if he did it intentionally, but there was this extraordinary symbolic moment of the young prince getting married and becoming the future king, and then him calling me and saying, "Off we go."'

Hiddleston was cast in three telefilms to be executive produced by the acclaimed English director Sam Mendes. In *Parts 1* and *2* of *Henry IV*, he would play Prince Hal, and in *Henry V* he would take the lead role. The three films would eventually be broadcast in 2012 as part of *The Hollow Crown* BBC2 series, along with a version of *Richard II*.

Once again, critics were comparing him to his friend and mentor Kenneth Branagh, who famously directed himself in his 1989 film of *Henry V*. He had in fact spoken at great length with Branagh about playing Henry V. When the seasoned actor found out Tom had been cast in the role, he sent him an email to congratulate him.

'He just said, "I heard about the Henrys. The very, very best of luck. You'll have a fantastic time,"' revealed Tom, who took the message as 'his blessing'.

'I do feel Shakespeare is like an Olympic torch that gets passed on from generation to generation.'

Tom described *Henry V* as being 'like Shakespeare's gladiator'. He explained the premise of the series to the BBC: 'They're part of a set of history plays that Shakespeare wrote about a sequence of English kings, starting with Richard II. He was deposed by Henry Bolingbroke, who became Henry IV. There's a civil war in Henry IV's reign, and upon his death his eldest son, Prince Hal, becomes Henry V.

'It's massive dynastic medieval history, injected with drama and the greatest poetry that's ever been written.'

He revelled in the opportunity to chart the journey of 'rebellious drunk' Prince Hal and his transformation to become king. When speaking to the entertainment and gossip website *Just Jared*, Tom described the Prince as being 'not what a prince should be. He's kind of out there, rocking it out, being a punk, and hanging in the pub with lowlifes and prostitutes'.

While filming the *Hollow Crown* series, Hiddleston told friends he was 'knee-deep in mud, blood and warrior poetry'. He knew there was no way he could match or complete with Laurence Olivier's famous portrayal of the

King in the 1944 Shakespearean film adaptation but he hoped to bring a new and refreshing approach to the role.

He would be starring alongside a stellar cast of actors including Jeremy Irons, John Hurt, Patrick Stewart, Ben Whishaw and Michelle Dockery. Just working with these people was in itself a great privilege. The series was planned to air alongside the BBC coverage of the London Olympics. It would form part of a season encompassing 12,000 events, reprising the idea of a cultural Olympiad. To fit in with the theme, Sam Mendes had chosen three Shakespearean plays about England.

The programmes garnered great interest from both the public and the media alike. Veteran TV presenter and journalist Jeremy Paxman invited Tom to appear on BBC2's *Newsnight* to take part in a discussion about political figures, comparing roles in medieval and modern times.

Tom appeared elegant and knowledgeable, eager to air his opinions and share his own astute observations. Demonstrating his knowledge and intelligence, he proved he was more than just a good actor and a pretty face.

'The interesting thing about *Henry V* is it dramatises that tussle between the responsibility of public office and the private torment of personal accountability very well,' he told Paxman. 'One of my favourite lines from the play is when, on the eve of Agincourt, Henry V disguised under the cloak of one of his captains gets into a debate with one of the soldiers about kingship and responsibility.

'This character Williams is casting various aspersions,

saying it will be a black matter when all those arms and legs are chopped off in battle, it will be a black matter for the king that led them to it. Henry's response is, "Every subject's duty is the King's. But every subject's soul is his own."'

When pressed as to why past monarchs held greater sway than their modern counterparts, Tom replied quickly with an eloquent and poignant answer: 'In our society we don't trust rhetoric in the same way. But another important thing to remember is that at that time the men and women in positions of power were also the same men and women leading their armies to battle. Henry V was able to give that speech then ride into battle himself, so in a way there's an authenticity to that rhetoric.'

He had read *Henry V* several times before, but this latest production allowed him to become much more intimately familiar with the character. It dawned on him just how often the play was misread and misunderstood. He complained to friends about 'lazy' interpretations. In his mind this was an 'incredibly brutal and violent piece of work examining the nature of warfare through the eyes of one man as he experiences it'.

After studying his character for some time, he felt inspired to write an article about Henry V for the *Radio Times*:

Henry V's victory at Agincourt is one of the most famous in English military history: the odds were against him; French outnumbered English by thousands, and Henry's men were dying of starvation and dysentery. Henry's victory was a feat of extraordinary individual bravery and impeccable and daring strategy.

What distinguished him, above all, were his qualities as a leader: his courage, his rhetoric, his authenticity, his self-sacrifice. 'We few, we happy few, we band of brothers'.

That I have been allowed to utter these immortal words on film is a source of great pride. Prince Hal/Henry V is one of Shakespeare's most fascinating characters, simply because the journey and arc of the character are so extreme and intense.

These films are about power and politics, princes and warrior poets. Shakespeare was the most compassionate and intelligent dramatist of his day. That compassion and intelligence still resonate in ours.

Once again, he expressed his enormous admiration for Shakespeare. He and Kenneth Branagh had discussed the brilliance of the playwright on many occasions. Every time Tom performed the Bard's works he felt honoured. Journalists were often amazed by his ability to spontaneously recite passages of plays. He would tell them: 'Shakespeare is our finest, most sophisticated, most extraordinary artistic legacy.

'Shakespeare had an enormous empathy not just about the man of the gutter, but of every man. That's why he's so extraordinary. He's able to think himself and feel himself in the minds of an entire people. Kings and queens are represented seemingly truthfully, as are men of the gutter.'

Although he had performed Shakespeare's plays on stage many times, acting in front of the cameras was a very different experience. In many ways there was a greater sense of realism: he was riding into actual battle.

The directors of the series were aware that one of the main challenges they faced was to make Shakespeare appealing and accessible to a mainstream TV audience. Although Tom found the language 'easily accessible and comprehensible', he appreciated others might struggle more to interpret the seemingly 'overly constructed, difficult and florid' copy.

'But the actor's job is to digest it, and then just speak it like you're making it up,' he told *Collider* website. 'Once you tune your ear to it, you pick everything up and it's gorgeous. It's like listening to great music.

'In a way, the great enemy to Shakespeare, for me, is people who have over-acted it and made it seem like this big, scary thing that you have to treat with great ceremony.'

He even managed to find elements of comedy in the plays. One of his favourite scenes involves Prince Hal 'taking the piss' out of warrior Harry Percy, the Hotspur, in the pub: 'He's drunk and he says, "I am not yet of Percy's mind, the Hotspur of the north, he that kills me some six or seven dozen Scots at a breakfast, washes his hands, and says to his wife, 'Fie upon this quiet life! I want work'."

'He's taking the piss out of him saying that he probably gets up and kills Scotsman for breakfast 'cause that's what he does. And that makes me laugh.'

Another of his favourite scenes in the play involves the moment the English army besiege a French castle by making a breach in the wall with a battering ram. But as the French issue a counterattack the English are sent running, leading Henry V to make one of his most stirring speeches.

'"In peace there nothing so becomes a man as modest stillness and humility. But when the blast of war blows in our ears, then imitate the action of the tiger."

'It's an extraordinary thing to say, "In peace time, be gentle, be kind, be humble. But when it's war, unleash the beast." That's what he's saying. You couldn't write it better than that,' Tom told *Collider*. 'I get very passionate about it because it just seems so modern. It seems like any coach in a locker room, or any group of underdogs who are down on their luck and seem to be facing some insurmountable obstacle. It fires me up.'

CHAPTER NINE

LOKI REVISITED

Playing Shakespeare allows an actor to fully flex his acting muscles and Tom received great praise for his performances in *The Hollow Crown* TV series. But it was his fantastical comic-strip character Loki who really wowed mainstream audiences.

Marvel Studios had made a fortune from their superhero film series and they were eager to build on that success. A plot of sci-fi stories and comic-book capers played out by an A-list cast was clearly a winning formula – the viewing public seemed to have an insatiable appetite for this type of film.

Thor, where Loki made his debut, had been one of the biggest summer hits when released in 2011. Worldwide, the film had taken in $450 million at the box office. Released in 2008 and directed by Jon Favreau, *Iron Man* had been the first superhero film in the Marvel Cinematic Universe (MCU) series. *Captain America: The First Avenger* (2011) had also been a great success. And so the studio decided it would be a clever idea to unite some of the popular characters in an ensemble film and came up with the plot line for Marvel *Avengers Assemble*, an animated TV series.

The original script was written by *The Incredible Hulk* screenwriter Zak Penn but he was replaced by *Buffy the Vampire Slayer* screenwriter and director Joss Whedon, who said the studio needed to 'pretend this draft never happened'. Whedon impressed Marvel Studios president Kevin Feige with an outline of what he thought *The Avengers* should be about, and he went away to compose a new script.

Loki would, of course, have a starring role. Tom was delighted to be invited back, describing the whole experience of playing Loki as 'entirely surreal'. He had had an inkling that he might be involved in the project, but had no idea in what capacity or to what extent until Whedon sent him a script a few months before filming was due to commence.

Some actors might squirm at the idea of reprising a role and covering similar territory, but for Hiddleston it was an absolute pleasure. He'd played such a broad variety of characters since first donning his leather suit and long black wig as Loki that he had no fears of being typecast; he was also fond of his growing legion of teenage fans. He had an admirable ability for juggling the role of cultured artist and blockbuster megastar.

'I feel so grateful,' he would say, enthused by the opportunity to play Loki again. 'It is so rare as an actor to be allowed the chance to revisit a role and to go back to a character that you already built, and lived inside, and understood,' he told the website *Collider*. 'To take it further to another stage is a huge privilege.'

He also knew that he owed a great deal to the long-haired villain. After all, it was Loki who had really made Tom Hiddleston a household name: 'It afforded me an extraordinary opportunity at a particular time. It's a great character. Lots of depth, lots of fun. The way he caught fire in the imagination of people is still completely surprising and gratifying.'

The new film was to star Robert Downey Jr., Chris Evans, Mark Ruffalo, Chris Hemsworth, Scarlett Johansson, Jeremy Renner, Clark Gregg and Samuel L. Jackson. The story revolved around Loki's attempt to invade Earth with the help of the Chitauri Army and Tesseract power; the Avengers must come together to save the planet from an alien invasion.

According to Amy Pascale's book *Joss Whedon: The Biography*, Tom wrote a heartfelt email after reading Whedon's draft for the first time:

Joss,

I am so excited I can hardly speak.

The first time I read it I grabbed at it like Charlie Bucket snatching for a golden ticket somewhere behind the chocolate in the wrapper of a Wonka Bar. I didn't know where to start. Like a classic actor I jumped in looking for LOKI on every page, jumping back and forth, reading words in no particular order, utterances imprinting themselves like flash-cuts of newspaper headlines in my mind: 'real menace'; 'field of obeisance'; 'discontented, nothing is enough'; 'his smile is nothing but a glimpse of his skull'; 'Puny god' ...

Thank you for writing me my Hans Gruber. But a Hans Gruber with super-magic powers. As played by James Mason ... It's high operatic villainy alongside detached throwaway tongue-in-cheek; plus the 'real menace' and his closely guarded suitcase of pain. It's grand and epic and majestic and poetic and lyrical and wicked and rich and badass and might possibly be the most gloriously fun part I've ever stared down the barrel of playing. It is just so juicy.

I love how throughout you continue to put Loki on some kind of pedestal of regal magnificence and then consistently tear him down. He gets battered, punched, blasted, side-swiped, roared at, sent tumbling on his back, and every time he gets back up smiling, wickedly, never for a second losing his eloquence, style, wit, self-aggrandisement or grandeur, and you never send him up or deny him his real intelligence.... That he loves to make an entrance; that he has a taste for the grand gesture, the big speech, the spectacle. I might be biased, but I do feel as though you have written me the coolest part.

But really I'm just sending you a transatlantic shout-out and fist-bump, things that traditionally British actors probably don't do. It's epic.

Whedon wrote back:

Tom, this is one of those emails you keep forever. Thanks so much. It's more articulate (and possibly longer) than the script. I couldn't be more pleased at your reaction, but I'll also tell you I'm still working on it ... Thank you again. I'm so glad you're pleased. Absurd fun to ensue.

Best, (including uncharacteristic fist-bump), Joss.

Speaking to *Empire* magazine about Loki's whereabouts between films, Tom explained: 'He's been lost in the dark recesses of the universe. It's like a superhero equivalent of getting lost in the jungle and he's come out the other side, scarred – internally and externally. He's more of a survivor. There was a regality to him in *Thor*, he was a lost prince. In *The Avengers* he's a maniac.

'In *Thor*, I was the god of misunderstood pain. In this film, I'm the god of mischief.'

Scarlett Johansson, who was cast as Natasha Romanoff aka Black Widow, said: 'Our characters have a long history. They've fought together for a long time in a lot of battles in many different countries. We're the two members of this avenging group who are skilled warriors – we have no superpowers.

'Black Widow is definitely one of the team, though. She's not in the cast simply to be a romantic foil or eye candy. She's there to fight, so I never felt like I was the only girl. We all have our various skills and it feels equal.'

To prepare for the role, the famously demure and attractive actress had to toughen up. 'I'd never done anything like that before. I'd never been physically driven in something, or a part of something so big,' she confessed.

She spent months training with the film's stunt team – 'fighting all the other actors'. 'It's crazy. I do nothing but fight – all the time,' she laughed.

One person who didn't have to work so hard to bulk up was beefcake Chris Hemsworth. He was able to maintain the physique he'd built up for his character Thor by eating his own 'body weight' in protein. His daily diet included chicken breasts, fish, steak and eggs.

He told *MTV*, 'Thor's motivation is much more of a personal one, in the sense that it's his brother that is stirring things up. Whereas everyone else, it's some bad guy who they've gotta take down. It's a different approach for me, or for Thor. He's constantly having to battle the greater good and what he should do vs. it's his little brother there. . . I've been frustrated with my brothers at times, or family, but I'm the only one who is allowed to be angry at them. There's a bit of that.'

Tom spent a great deal of time contemplating his character's development. The thing he loved most about Loki was the scope of the character: 'There is almost no ceiling to his complexity!' he exclaimed to *Collider* in 2012.

Shortly after he had finished filming *Thor*, he'd had a meeting with Joss Whedon, who already knew he'd be directing *The Avengers*. Whedon was keen to know exactly how Loki's mind ticked.

'Tell me everything about living inside of this man for six months. Tell me what makes him tick, what keeps him up at night. What are the nightmares of his soul?' he asked Tom. The two men had a long discussion about Norse mythology, comic books and the approach Hiddleston had developed with Kenneth Branagh. Whedon was impressed.

'He loved it and he loved all of those ideas,' Tom told the website *Collider* in 2012. 'He loved all of Loki's damage and that somewhere at the bottom of Loki's credentials as a bad guy he is a searching spirit. He is a damaged soul searching for the answers to something. Why he exists, what is his role in this universe, that he isn't just somebody who is evil for the sake of being evil. He has complicated reasons for that.'

Both were aware of the risks of saturating the market with superhero films. They agreed this movie had to be different: how could they make it distinctive and unique?

Whedon decided to give each character his own individual pain and focused on the healing powers afforded by working together as a group: 'I think the Loki we see in *The Avengers* is further advanced. You have to ask yourself the question: How pleasant an experience is it disappearing into a wormhole that has been created by some kind of super nuclear explosion of his own making? So I think by the time Loki shows up in *The Avengers*, he's seen a few things.

'I think that what was interesting about the journey of Loki in *Thor* is that he went from second string and damaged prince to being the God of mischief and God of evil. I think somewhere between the end of *Thor* and the beginning of *The Avengers*, Loki has been to the Marvel equivalent of the 7th circle of hell.

'At the end of *Thor* you see him let go. He lets go of the spear, he lets go of Asgard, and he lets go of the need of his brother and father's affection and approval. He has bigger plans now.

'The Loki of *Thor* is a confused and damaged prince and the Loki of *The Avengers* is somebody who understands his own power,' he told *Collider* in 2012.

Meanwhile Tom reached the conclusion that his character could now manage and even suppress his own anger: 'Loki is the God of mischief and I think that the way Joss has written Loki in *The Avengers* is that he is a mischief. He is someone whose actions are very, very difficult for the seven of eight Avengers to pin down.'

When discussing plot lines with the *Hollywood Reporter* he revealed: 'At the beginning of *The Avengers*, he [Loki] comes to Earth to subjugate it and his idea is to rule the human race as their king. And like all the delusional autocrats of human history, he thinks this is a great idea because if everyone is busy worshipping him, there will be no wars so he will create some kind of world peace by ruling them as a tyrant.

'But he is also kind of deluded in the fact that he thinks unlimited power will give him self-respect, so I haven't let go of the fact that he is still motivated by this terrible jealousy and kind of spiritual desolation.'

Tom felt it would be a great shame to play a character that was 'all out evil', instead preferring to retain the complexities and different dimensions he'd developed in *Thor*. He concluded Loki felt unloved, abandoned and alone; 'like any completely delusional fascist in the course of human history' he was suffering a lack of self-esteem. Through power, he hoped to earn approval and self-respect.

'He's a tough nut to crack!' he admitted.

Filming alongside so many A-list actors could be slightly overwhelming. Tom never once felt out of his depth but he did appreciate the good company he was keeping. Besides, if he ever felt nervous he only had to consider how ridiculous they all looked in their sci-fi outfits.

'There was one day when, as Loki, I was sat on some steps, staring at the Avengers in front of me. But the fact that they were dressed in the most outlandish hero costumes was bizarre! And I thought to myself, "This is the dizzy heights," he told the *Independent* in 2012.

Looking back, he would later rate the first day of filming *The Avengers* as 'definitely one of the great moments of my life' – 'A bunch of fully grown adults, most of whom were stonking great movie stars, all pointing and laughing at each other.

'"Look at you in your Spandex!" "Well, look at you in *your* Spandex!"'

Although Tom had worked with several of the cast members before, he quickly acquainted himself with everyone involved in the project. There was a real sense of fun and camaraderie on set. The actors spent a great deal of time on location in Albuquerque, New Mexico. He described the experience to *Just Jared* in 2011 as being 'like camp' – 'You kind of band together because nobody's got anywhere else to be. No one's got home to go to, so it's like, "Does anyone wanna play some ping-pong after work?"'

In fact, many hours off-camera were spent playing table tennis. Tom confessed he enjoyed nothing more than 'a marathon round of table tennis': 'I've got to say, Captain America (Chris Evans) and Thor (Chris Hemsworth), they might have bigger biceps than me, but put them on the table tennis table. There's a degree of frustration at their inability to beat me.'

Meanwhile Scarlett Johansson joked to journalists that Tom was 'clinically enthusiastic'.

'Tom is my absolute hero,' she giggled. 'Doing a scene with him is like playing tennis with Venus Williams. He's just always there to hit the ball back no matter which direction it's coming from. He's got a powerful serve!'

She also warned that he had a 'secret sweet tooth' –

'I've never seen anyone devour sugar the way he does,' she remarked.

Tom also had good words to say about his co-star. He thoroughly enjoyed filming scenes with her. 'I loved playing my scene with Scarlett, because Black Widow is sneaky, underhand, and she lurks in the shadows,' he told *Collider* in 2012.

'She is smart, clever, and duplicitous and she's hard to trust. All of those adjectives could also be used to describe Loki. So the scene between Loki and Black Widow is one where they recognize each other.'

Off-screen, by Tom's own admission, the pair became 'good friends': 'We went horse riding in the desert,' he revealed to a Russian TV interviewer. 'She's a good horse rider.'

But when the journalist commented on how romantic the idea sounded, Tom bristled: 'Friends can go horse riding too.'

It was all too tempting to imagine sparks might fly between the attractive pair, but Tom had nothing but words of respect and admiration for the actress although he did admit she looked good in a catsuit.

'That catsuit on Scarlett is something else!' he swooned to an American chat show host. 'She's not just OK in a catsuit – she's astonishing. She's gorgeous – on the inside and outside – and she kicks arse in this movie! She trained and trained.

'Chris Hemsworth and Chris Evans were born that way, genetically modified. But she trained and trained.'

But when asked who had the best butt on set, Tom joked: 'Chris Evans by a mile – the guy's rocking it for Spandex. I expect Spandex sales to go through the roof!'

Samuel L. Jackson also enjoyed working with Tom, and had only praise for the actor, telling GQ in 2013 'He's prepared and that's important for me. He's a guy who's ready to go and he has a plan. He's open to what the other actors are doing, very complementary to the other talent around him in terms of giving them something to work with and returning something when you give it to him.

'A lot of actors are like blank pages: you write on them and nothing happens. Tom is very responsive.'

In return, Hiddleston also had only good things to say about his fellow actor: 'Samuel L. Jackson was a hero of mine as a teenager and to suddenly be in a scene with him was extraordinary.'

Considering the number of A-list stars in the cast, it was surprising how down-to-earth everyone behaved; there were no diva antics on set and they all had the same-sized trailer. Plus, everyone was willing to help each other or to share tips on how to approach a scene.

'The thing that distinguishes actors of any strike is their generosity; they're not possessive of their gift.'

Tom had thoroughly enjoyed working with Kenneth Branagh, so director Joss Whedon had a tough act to follow. But Tom respected his different approach to the franchise, describing him to friends as an 'amazing director'.

'Joss has kind of got this pan-literacy about the genre

and his dexterity in negotiating all the different story lines, all the different characters, all the different tones just so that it's real and relatable and funny and dynamic and then just badass, because that's what *The Avengers* has to be!' he told the website *Just Jared* in 2011.

'So he was capable of directing intensely dynamic scenes between two characters, but also delivering action on the most incredible scale. I can't say enough about Joss.'

Whedon in turn had an appreciation for British theatre and respected Tom's experience of acting onstage. In between takes the pair would often start chatting about their favourite British theatre actors and stage shows. Joss even told Tom he'd almost become a theatre director. Like Branagh, he was also a big fan of Shakespeare. The two men had very different methods of working, but Tom could appreciate them equally.

Although off-camera some fantastic friendships were blossoming, it was a very different story for the characters on set. There were plenty of high-octane fight scenes and Tom thrived on the adrenaline of filming physical encounters.

'I loved doing all of the fight stuff,' he told the website *Collider*. 'I think what was so thrilling about the fights that we have already shot and choreographed is that R.A. Rondell, who is the stunt coordinator on the film, has really embraced the different physicality and superpowers of every character. Chris Hemsworth has his hammer and the size of his arms. Chris Evans has his shield and Scarlett as Black Widow has been doing a lot of wuxia stuff. Robert has his suit and Loki has his intelligence and his ability to disappear and reappear and his staff. So I think the fights will be really thrilling to watch.'

To prepare for the physical scenes, Tom made an effort to get fit and bulk up. 'There was always a worry expressed amongst comic book enthusiasts that if Thor could defeat Loki in the *Thor* film then why would he need *The Avengers* to help defeat him?' he revealed. 'We knew we had to dial up the intensity of his menace.'

As soon as Hiddleston arrived in Albuquerque, he hit the gym. After all, he was in the middle of the desert so there was little else to occupy his downtime off camera. 'We have the greatest stunt team in the world led by R.A. Rondell and Jon Eusebio,' he told friends.

There was no excuse not to pull his weight!

His rigorous training involved doing several kinds of martial arts, including Wushu, boxing, lots of stick and staff work, knife work and hand-to-hand combat. 'There were also a lot of daily repetition drills that condition your body and muscle memory,' he told the *comicbookmovie* website. 'That's how you learn to jump off a building, fly through the air, barely miss Chris Hemsworth's head and get slammed to the ground on your back, pick yourself up and repeat the same motion 12 times over the course of a day in a costume of leather and metal that weighs forty pounds.'

Besides, this wasn't just an opportunity to get in shape; working out also helped him to get to grips with the intricacies of Loki's character – 'I started going through the movements and as I did more and more, I started reconnecting to the character because I believe how you move informs everyone of who you are.'

In spite of all the hard work Tom put in at the gym, he still managed to walk away from set with a few cuts and bruises.

'I have bruises all over my body, but it's called "The Avengers" and if it wasn't action-packed, we've failed to do our jobs!' he declared.

One of the biggest battles involved a clash between Loki and Thor on top of the Stark Tower. 'Thor uses his hammer like a boxing glove and Loki uses his sceptre in more of a Wushu way,' explained Tom. 'But after a little bit, Thor drops his hammer, Loki drops his sceptre, and it's just two brothers fighting sloppy and nasty.'

Fight choreographer Jonathan Eusebio added: 'Thor wants to take Loki home without harming him, while Loki wants to approach the fight with deadly intentions. As the fight continues, emotions escalate and the stakes get bigger. Thor becomes really angry and the fight becomes very brutal at its conclusion.'

In truth, Tom loved the fight scenes. Surprisingly, though, his pleasure derived not from some deep-seated machismo, but simply because he viewed them as an art form: 'I love shooting action because my brain switches off and it's almost like a dance once you get the moves down.

'All you have to do then is add in the emotion of throwing or catching a punch and it almost becomes a very Zen-like experience. So by the time you get to the day of shooting a fight between Loki and Captain America, hopefully the preparation and training kick in and it becomes about the simplicity of execution.'

Plus he hated the idea of using a stunt double: 'As a cinephile and movie lover, I get such a kick when you see an actor flying across the screen and you know that it's the real actor who's done the stunt. I hate when they just cut around a stunt double and you just see the back of the actor's head. I don't want to see the back of my head, so I am always ready to get in there and mix it up with the stunt team.'

He described the whole period of filming in New Mexico as 'really relaxed and chilled'. Being so remote, the team were rarely troubled by paparazzi. It was only when they filmed the final few scenes in New York's Central Park that the magnitude of the project really dawned on him – 'It went crazy. I realised then that I was in a big movie.'

Although there were huge expectations surrounding the release of the film, Tom refused to be phased by the outcome. Loki had gathered such a big fan base, there was always a risk people might be disappointed by his latest portrayal. But he refused to think that way: all he could do was focus on the role and do his best. That had always been his approach.

'It's my responsibility to play this guy and his version of the truth is my responsibility. What other people see in that representation is up to them,' he insisted.

CHAPTER TEN

COMIC-CON

Despite the success of the Marvel franchise, some critics continued to dismiss the superhero movies as superficial blockbuster pap. Tom Hiddleston strongly disagreed. He'd spent hours, weeks – even years – exploring the complexities of his character, Loki. There was far greater depth to the films than perhaps many could initially imagine.

Tom felt so strongly about the subject, he penned an article for the *Guardian* newspaper, published on 19 April 2012. He introduced the piece by recounting a conversation he'd had with the actor Malcolm Sinclair. While the pair were tucking into early-morning scrambled eggs during a break in filming, Sinclair told him a story about Christopher Reeve. When Reeve accepted the role of Superman, he became a subject of mockery amongst friends on Broadway – it wasn't the sort of thing a classical actor would do.

Tom couldn't believe it. He'd always held Christopher Reeve in high esteem; he loved Superman. 'I grew up watching *Superman*,' he wrote. 'As a child, when I first learned to dive into a swimming pool, I wasn't diving, I was flying, like Superman. I used to dream of rescuing a girl I had a crush on (my Lois Lane) from a playground bully (General Zod). Reeve, to my mind, was the first real superhero.'

He went on to list the number of actors who have 'turned superheroes into a serious business' and praised Heath Ledger for his game-changing performance as the Joker in *The Dark Knight* (2008), describing it as 'dark, anarchic, dizzying, free, and totally, thrillingly, dangerous'.

He believed a number of worldly truths could be communicated through superhero films: 'In our increasingly secular society, with so many disparate gods and different faiths, superhero films present a unique canvas upon which our shared hopes, dreams and apocalyptic nightmares can be projected and played out.'

And he compared Marvel's characters to the great gods of classical stories, their tales acting as allegories for the grander journey of human existence. The Hulk was a metaphor for anger; Captain America was a war hero; Spider-Man was an embodiment of 'independent thought and power'.

The ideas were lofty, but his eloquent explanations were remarkably down-to-earth and made sense. He also praised the films for their thrilling chase sequences, drawing on a tradition dating back to the beginning of cinema.

'Maybe playing superheroes isn't such an ignoble undertaking after all,' he concluded. '"I still believe in heroes," says Samuel L. Jackson's Nick Fury in *Avengers Assemble*. So do I, sir. So do I.'

A week later, *Avengers Assemble* was released in UK cinemas. It was a hit with fans and grossed more than $1.5 billion at the box office worldwide, making it the highest-grossing film of 2012. Review aggregator website *Rotten Tomatoes* reported the film had an average 92 per cent approval rating with an average of 8 out of 10 (based on 315 reviews).

They summarised: 'Thanks to a script that emphasizes its heroes' humanity and a wealth of super-powered set pieces, *The Avengers* lives up to its hype and raises the bar for Marvel at the movies.'

Rolling Stone journalist Peter Travers said it was the epitome of the perfect blockbuster: 'It's *Transformers* with a brain, a heart and a working sense of humour.'

The movie would go on to receive an Academy Award nomination for Best Visual Effects and a British Academy Film Award nomination for Best Special Visual Effects.

Many of the actors praised Joss Whedon for his script, which he'd totally rewritten. He claimed the original script, a draft written by Zak Penn, was disastrous. In *Joss Whedon: The Biography* by Amy Pascale he regales an initial interview with Kevin Feige, president of production at Marvel Studios, where Whedon told Feige: 'You need to pretend this draft never happened.'

'There was a script,' he later told *GQ* magazine. 'There just wasn't a script I was going to film a word of.'

Whedon said he could only work on a script he believed in, so he went away to draft his own version. Disney gave him a required outline – which included keeping Loki in the picture – but also allowed him the freedom to be creative with the plot.

* * *

Marvel's franchise was growing from strength to strength, and it wasn't long before Tom was signed up for the next instalment, *Thor 2*, which would eventually be released in 2013 as *Thor: The Dark World*.

Hiddlestoners had already been pleading with Marvel to let Loki have his own spin-off movie.

'Who knows?' Tom said wryly when quizzed by reporters.

If the studio bosses needed any further persuasion they only had to look at the response the actor received when he appeared at Comic-Con International 2013. Held from 18–21 July at the San Diego Convention Center, the annual event attracted huge crowds. Since its inception in 1970, according to *Forbes* it had grown to become the largest convention of its kind anywhere in the world. Along with talks, toys and video game demonstrations, it also served as a platform for directors to reveal teasers of new projects.

Marvel Studios president Kevin Feige intended to use it as an opportunity to present footage from the upcoming

Thor movie but just as he started to address the audience the lights went out and they were plunged into darkness.

'Humanity, look how far you've fallen,' came a familiar voice from the shadows. 'Lining up in the sweltering heat for hours. Huddling together in the dark like beasts.'

As the studio lights came up, Tom Hiddleston was revealed in his full Loki regalia.

'Loki! Loki!' chanted the audience of screaming fans.

Putting a finger to his lips to usher some silence, Tom continued: 'I am Loki and I am burdened with glorious purpose.

'The bright lure of freedom diminishes your life's joy in a mad scramble for a place in this chamber – in this arena they call Hall H.

'You should have let me rule you when you had the chance. Your ears yearn untold stories, your eyes crave unseen sights, your imaginations ache and hunger. Where are your Avengers now?

'Say my name.

'It seems I have an army.

'Feast your eyes!'

By now the crowd was charged and frenzied. It no longer really mattered what the footage showed, they were pumped for the next instalment.

Tom was amazed by the response. Adrenaline surged through his bloodstream. Never before, in all his years of acting, had he ever experienced anything quite like this.

'I went to drama school to train as a stage actor, but to

six-and-a-half-thousand strong? That's the biggest gig I've ever played for sure!' he told journalists afterwards.

'It was incredible. Crazy. Deranged and all out bananas. I wanted it to be good and to work. I had no idea that would be the response when I walked out on stage.

'I didn't know that they were going to start saying my name, before I told them to. It was really, really fun. It was more fun than should be allowed.'

He even compared the experience to being like Glastonbury – 'I understand why Mick Jagger does that kind of thing at 70 years old. It's a rush!'

And drawing on his knowledge of Shakespeare he said: 'I was confronted with a wall of sound and fury.'

This was only Tom's second visit to Comic-Con. He'd visited three years previously, in 2010, with Kenneth Branagh, Kat Dennings, Chris Hemsworth and Natalie Portman. At that point no one was really familiar with the character of Thor. Now, of course, it was a totally different experience.

The idea for the skit was borne out of a conversation with Kevin Feige about a month previously. He'd called Tom and suggested he come to the convention in character. The pair discussed ideas over email and several phone conversations.

'I knew I didn't want to break character, I wanted to be Loki,' Tom explained to the press. 'Otherwise I'd unknit all the work I've done over the past three films. But my God, it was fun. I couldn't hear anything, I couldn't see. When I walked out on stage there were so many flashes in my face. It felt like the end of *Raiders of the Lost Ark*, when all the Nazis are having their eyes blown out. It was a riot, a hoot.'

In order to make the sequence work it was important no one knew Hiddleston was attending the convention. Even his co-stars had no clue what was about to happen.

'It was basically a top-secret stealth mission by Kevin and myself,' revealed Tom. 'Nobody else knew about it. Kevin just said to everyone else, "We're not doing a panel, we're just going to show the trailer."'

Eager not to attract any attention, Tom arrived at the convention in disguise – he really wanted the whole episode to be a surprise. He flew in from London to San Diego dressed as Jango Fett from the *Star Wars* movies. Had he arrived in plain clothes, someone would be bound to post a picture on social media.

'But why Jango Fett?' asked one journalist.

'I'm six foot two,' replied Tom. 'It was the only one that fit in the costume shop – they were sold out of Stormtroopers.'

After quietly arriving through Security, he rushed to his hotel, where he remained in hiding. 'I was in lock-down,' he confessed. 'I was living like Julian Assange! I couldn't leave the hotel, I couldn't leave my room.'

Once again, he was overwhelmed by the response from his fans.

'I'm so proud,' he gushed. 'I never dreamed that I would ever create a character that was so loved, or whatever he is! I'm not quite sure whether he's loved, but people are fascinated by him; they seem to enjoy his existence. It's cool.'

Much as he'd enjoyed the performance, it wasn't a spectacle he was planning to repeat in a hurry, though: 'I hope to high heaven that I never give a performance of that scale onscreen. It was big, shall we say. I'm used to working with directors who say less is more, whereas yesterday it was kind of a 21-gun salute,' he told reporters.

'As a live performer, I never forget that. It's a very unique thing. You don't get it onscreen with a camera. A camera is something you have to project that charge onto. It doesn't come for free. It's a mechanical, technological entity. Whereas with an audience, it's a chemistry; you can feel something coming off them.'

Although at times it could be daunting, he would never underestimate the power of that energy: 'The energy that comes towards me is incredibly passionate, but completely benign and very generous. An actor can't call himself an actor unless there's an audience.'

* * *

Directed by Alan Taylor, with a screenplay by Christopher Yost, *Thor: The Dark World* (2013) starred Chris Hemsworth, Natalie Portman, Anthony Hopkins, Stellan Skarsgård, Idris Elba, Christopher Eccleston, Adewale Akinnuoye-Agbaje, Kat Dennings, Ray Stevenson, Zachary Levi, Tadanobu Asano, Jaimie Alexander, Rene Russo and, of course, Tom Hiddleston.

In the film, Thor and Loki team up to save the Nine Realms from the Dark Elves, who are threatening to take over the universe. Initially, Kenneth Branagh had been involved in the project but he withdrew in the very early stages.

Tom described the sequel as: 'enormous, epic, challenging'.

'Chris Hemsworth and I wanted to do something new. A new journey and iteration for the characters – that their natures evolve and change. It has all the good stuff and some new stuff.'

He shared his thoughts with Kevin Feige, who sought advice from the star on how the character of Loki should be developed. Towards the end of filming for *Avengers Assemble*, the pair had spent many hours together in airport lounges, discussing what might happen next.

'I'm genuinely grateful for his open-mindedness and collaboration,' said Tom. 'I feel very trusted by him as someone who has an input into Loki.'

He recalled saying to Feige and Chris Hemsworth: 'Loki and Thor have been antagonists for two films. We can't do that again. Wouldn't it be amazing if they fought side by side for whatever reason in whatever complicated allegiance? It would still be great if somehow they had to overcome their differences and fight a common enemy. There'd be a lot of drama and tension and comedy that could come out of that thing.'

Feige agreed and the idea ended up being the basis of the movie.

Tom even wrote a scene into the film when a guard comes to tell Loki about the death of another character. 'That scene didn't exist before,' he told reporters. 'It's in the movie and I'm really proud of it.'

The incredible response to Hiddleston's appearance at Comic-Con led the directors to write a new scene into *Thor*, although it never actually made the final cut. 'There was an idea to begin the film with an echo of the coronation at the beginning of Kenneth Branagh's *Thor*,' Tom explained. The fantasy sequence featured Loki holding the Mjölnir, Thor's hammer.

'It somehow played into his sense of displacement from his family, his rejection by them. That he got to be top dog in that situation.'

Having played Loki several times, he felt he knew the character well and he had a lot invested in the role. He appreciated the fact Marvel Studios had acknowledged that. It would have been very easy for them to simply send him a script and tell him to follow it verbatim. Instead, there was a great deal of collaboration on set; it was a work in progress.

Tom revelled in having creative input but he was quick to add that he wasn't the only one contributing ideas – 'Like all great collaborations, the best are those who rise to the time and that's what's in the film.'

During the filming of *Avengers*, Joss Whedon had encouraged Tom to enjoy himself, bringing some light relief to the character of Loki: 'He's having a good time teasing

Above left: Tom's big break – pictured with his Best Newcomer Award for his dual role as Cloten and Posthumus in Cheek by Jowl's theatre production of *Cymbeline* at the 2008 Laurence Olivier Awards. *(© Yui Mok PA Archive/PA Images)*

Above right: Stephen Spielberg and Hiddleston at the premiere of *War Horse* at the Lincoln Center in New York, December 2011. *(© Graylock ABACA USA/PA Images)*

Below: Hiddleston as Loki, Chris Hemsworth as Thor, Jeremy Renner as Hawkeye, Scarlett Johansson as Black Widow, Chris Evans as Captain America, Robert Downey Jr. as Iron Man and Mark Ruffalo as The Hulk on the set of *The Avengers* in Central Park, New York, September 2011.

(© IKN ABACA USA/PA Images)

Above left: With Marvel author and creator Stan Lee at the premiere of the original *Thor* film in Los Angeles, May 2011.　*(© Kevin Winter/Getty Images)*

Above right: Winning the Glamour Man of the Year Award in May 2012 – his role as Loki in the Marvel films had firmly placed him among the movers and shakers of Hollywood.　*(© Ian West PA Archive/PA Images)*

Below: Hiddleston arriving with Loki fans at the world premiere of *Thor: The Dark World* in London, October 2013.　*(© Ian West PA Archive/PA Images)*

Above left: Hiddleston, Olivia Colman, Elizabeth Debicki and Hugh Laurie at the premiere of *The Night Manager* in Los Angeles, April 2016.

(© LuMarPHOTO AFF/PA Images)

Above right: Hiddleston with Taylor Swift during the height of their short-lived relationship, leaving LAX airport for Australia where Tom was filming the new *Thor* movie, July 2016. *(©GC Images/Getty Images)*

Below: Hiddleston with his friend and mentor Kenneth Branagh, at the 62nd *Evening Standard* Theatre Awards at The Old Vic Theatre, London, November 2016. *(© David M. Benett/Getty Images)*

Above: Hiddleston posing with his Golden Globe for Best Actor in a TV Series for his role in *The Night Manager*, January 2017.   *(© Hahn Lionel/ABACA USA/PA Images)*

Below: The next blockbuster – Hiddleston, Brie Larson and Samuel L. Jackson at the *Kong: Skull Island* premiere in London, February 2017.

(Chris J Ratcliffe PA Wire/PA Images)

everybody and playing everyone else off each other like a chess master. And now I really feel like I'm the god of mischief. And playing that mischievous element in all its unpredictability is really, really fun,' Hiddleston declared.

Indeed his enjoyment of Loki's devilishness is something Alan Taylor really liked and wanted to keep. The director would say to him: 'You are toying with these people, so let's keep it.'

When discussing the approach he'd adopted for playing Loki a third time, Tom revealed: 'My compass, or guiding principle this time was evolution, development, and expansion in every respect. I was very keen not to repeat myself, and to try and find new ways to keep Loki engaging, entertaining, and interesting.'

Tom loved the new complexities his character had been afforded. He had two extremes to his personality; he was both playful and destructive: 'If you look up mischief in the dictionary, the first entry is an inclination to playfulness or to tease. And then somewhere down the line are destruction and damage.'

In that time he had grown extremely fond of his character, describing him as both nasty and elegant – 'He's someone who looks good doing really bad things.'

He felt this film marked a new chapter too: 'The last time Loki was in Asgard was at the end of *Thor* when he let go of the spear and he disappeared into a wormhole in space and time. And then he spent a degree of time on earth trying to destroy New York. And now he's back in Asgard a different being with a different mind-set. And therefore the kind of chemistry that he created just by being back there is unpredictable and fantastic.'

Tom also loved having the opportunity to work with Chris Hemsworth again. Since making *Thor* several years previously, the two men had become friends. They had first met at Kenneth Branagh's house in 2009. 'We had this amazing moment of mutual recognition,' Hiddleston recalls. 'We were both in our late twenties; we both had been kicking around for a while, and had opportunities and had missed them. But here was this incredible chance to make something great, and to work with these great actors, and great directors.'

Since then both had gone on to do some fantastic projects. Tom had enormous respect for Hemsworth and described him as a magnificent actor.

'Working with Chris for the third time was incredible,' he said. 'He's probably the greatest scene partner I've ever had and there is a complete trust between us. Having gone on this journey together across these three films, they're huge experiences.'

Tom had many memorable moments from shooting the *Thor* sequel. One of his favourite scenes was filmed on location in Iceland: 'We were shooting on top of a volcano in Iceland. There was a fight sequence where Loki has to take a big hit. He's sort of thrown back and falls on to the ground. I did a real-life high jump, I took a run-up to a mark, did a Fosbury Flop and then, smack… on to the surface of the volcano! Then I saw the shot afterwards and whatever was happening in my face, I could never have acted that.'

The film also contained one of his favourite lines ever uttered by Loki: 'Thor says to Loki, "I wish I could trust you." Loki's response is, "If you did you'd be the fool I always took you for. Trust my rage."'

By all accounts, and true to its title, this was a much darker film. 'It's not just about the mythological and physical battle between dark and light,' explained Tom to reporters. 'But there's something about growing up and accepting responsibility no matter who you are.

'Whether you are a crowned king, a king in waiting or a shamed prisoner, accepting responsibility and growing up is dark. It's a dark experience.'

Another co-star who captured Tom's imagination was Natalie Portman. He even interviewed her for *Elle* magazine. 'Natalie Portman has a neat right hook,' he wrote. 'I know this because the first time we shared screen time, she punched me in the face.'

Ben Cooke, fight coordinator on *Thor: The Dark World*, had given both actors some coaching in preparation for the scene. 'Go for it. Tom's a big guy, he can handle it,' he told Portman, who was playing the film's heroine, American astrophysicist Jane Foster.

Four times out of five, she gave him a close shave, but missed – which is the intention. But on the last round she accidentally connected her fist with Hiddleston's chin.

'The real thing, I'm pleased to say, is in the film,' wrote Tom.

He went on to praise her sense of humour on set. Portman was always the first one to start giggling, amused by the ridiculousness of adults dressed in Spandex, attempting to save the world in a fibre-glass spaceship. Her laughter was infectious, and on many occasions she would send the whole room into fits of giggles.

Tom had first met the actress in 2008, when he was appearing at the Donmar Warehouse in a production of Shakespeare's *Othello*. Natalie had come backstage to the dressing rooms to see her friend Ewan McGregor, who was starring in the play. The pair met again in 2010, on the set of Kenneth Branagh's original *Thor*, although they didn't actually get to work together as their characters never appeared together on screen. But they briefly met at Branagh's house. Unfortunately, Tom had been for a run with Chris Hemsworth and they were both 'wearing (accidentally) matching Nike gear, out of breath and drenched in sweat'.

When Tom arranged to meet Natalie for his *Elle* interview in LA, he arrived several hours late after being stuck in traffic. But when he found Portman sitting in a booth at Middle Eastern restaurant Carousel, surrounded by bowls of hummus and plates of salad, she was happy to see him.

In a display of characteristic diligence Tom had rewatched all of Natalie's films in preparation for the interview. One of his favourites was *Léon: The Professional* (1994), which he hadn't seen since he was fourteen.

Tom asked the actress about feminism, being a mum and her love of *Dirty Dancing*! He recalled a moment on the set of *Thor: The Dark World* when Chris Hemsworth had recited the script of *Point Break* in its entirety. This had led to a discussion about Patrick Swayze and, of course, *Dirty Dancing*.

Natalie had replied: 'Be very careful what you say about *Dirty Dancing*, because it has formed my soul.'

She ended the interview by revealing that she'd very much enjoyed punching Loki – 'Oh my God! It was so good.'

'I'm pleased to have given pleasure in some regard,' Tom joked in response. 'Even if it is just to have been a target for Natalie's unprocessed rage.'

Joking apart, the pair had become good friends.

'Tom is wonderful,' Natalie said. 'He's just an incredible actor who finds so much humour in his evil. He's also fun to be around, and he and Chris [Hemsworth] have a great rapport with each other. They've got sort of a brotherly thing. They really enjoy each other and annoy each other in a loving, joking way. It's fun to be around.'

* * *

By now Tom had starred alongside so many A-listers, but never once was he star-struck. In fact, the only time he was ever fazed by meeting a famous person was at Wimbledon – 'I tend to get star-struck by tennis players. I was at Wimbledon and I met Boris Becker. When I was a kid he was the greatest tennis player in the world. Now he's a commentator and I really enjoy listening to him,' he said.

When *Thor: The Dark World* was eventually released, once again Hiddleston was amazed by the response from fans. At the German premiere, one Loki fan even asked him to kneel before her – and so he did.

'I do have an army of amazing fans and supporters,' Tom admitted. 'I'm very privileged. But when the going gets tough, I lean on my sisters and my best friends. They make me laugh.'

Even though he'd had ample time to get used to the idea, he still couldn't get to grips with the notion of being a celebrity. Instead he preferred to emulate the attitude of actors he held in high esteem: people like Kenneth Branagh, Anthony Hopkins and Judi Dench who refused to be distracted by such things. Tom preferred to block out tabloid tales as 'white noise' – he just wanted to focus on the project in hand.

CHAPTER ELEVEN

CORIOLANUS, MUPPETS & MORE

*T*hor: *The Dark World* premiered at the Odeon Leicester Square in London on 22 October 2013. It was a commercial success, grossing more than $644 million worldwide, but the reviews were mixed.

Review website *Rotten Tomatoes* reported a 66 per cent approval rating with an average rating of 6.2 out of 10 based on 245 reviews. Justin Chang of *Variety* wrote: 'This robust, impersonal visual-effects showpiece proves buoyant and unpretentious enough to offset its stew of otherwise derivative fantasy/action elements.'

Ben Child of the *Guardian* said: 'Thanks to Hiddleston and Hemsworth's impressive collective charisma, *Thor: The Dark World* is far from a franchise killer.'

Meanwhile Jeannette Catsoulis of *The New York Times*

noted: 'The battle scenes are as lacking in heat and coherence as the central love story.'

The movie may not have met with critical approval, but as far as the fans were concerned it was a hit. Sadly for Loki fans though, it looked as if the next Marvel Studios instalment would not star Tom Hiddleston.

'I think it's great for *Avengers 2* that I'm not going to be in it,' Tom told journalists in a press conference. 'I'm so proud of the first one. If I was in it, we'd be chasing that again. The Avengers need new bad guys to fight.

'I'll miss the dance parties and Scarlett [Johansson] mixes a mean tequila, but I'll be waving them off and I'll be in the front row when it comes out!'

* * *

Although Tom would miss working with the team, he was pleased to have the opportunity to focus on new projects. He had enjoyed focusing on the superhero genre and having the opportunity to refine his character, but he knew it was time to get back to his first love – Shakespeare.

Filming *The Hollow Crown* BBC TV film series had reignited his interest in The Bard. 'It was actually doing these films that made me realize that, as soon as I possibly could, I had to find a moment to get back,' he told *Collider* website.

'The text and the writing is so rich, and the feelings are so big. Shakespeare is basically drawing in the biggest shapes available, as a writer, and with the most breathtaking language that's ever been written.'

Filming the BBC programmes had been enjoyable, but the turnaround had been quick: each film was shot in just four and a half weeks. Now he yearned for an opportunity to invest more time in his characters.

'The beauty of Shakespeare is that it's so rich that you go to bed at night and you wake yourself up thinking, "Tonight, I'm going to try this. I'm going to try this idea. I'm going to try to expand this metaphor or address it to this character or play it bigger and broader." And then, maybe the next day, I'll play it smaller.'

He knew the only place he could indulge such fantasies was in the theatre.

His stunt at Comic-Con had reminded him of the important role an audience played. 'An actor is nothing without his audience,' he told himself. 'So often, in the theatre, audiences don't know that they are complicit in the chemistry of the show that night. Their quality of listening and their quality of engagement always enhances or diminishes the show itself because we can feel it. It's a real relationship. And I love that.'

He could read the same script and play the same role a thousand times but he relished the fact no one performance would ever be the same. The audience was extremely influential in that.

Tom's next stage role was in *Coriolanus* at his old stomping ground the Donmar Warehouse. One of Shakespeare's lesser-known plays, the Roman drama is a tragedy of political manipulation and revenge. Rome is under threat and the legendary leader Caius Marcius Coriolanus is called on to defend the grand city. But famine and civil unrest cause untold problems for the protagonist when he returns home from the battlefield.

'It's about the greatest general in the Roman army, who becomes a national hero and so is corralled by the elite to become a politician,' Tom explained to the *Evening Standard* in 2013. 'But he's not equipped for politics, he's equipped for soldiery. It plays upon this very true characteristic of human nature, how we build people up and then we tear them down.'

The Donmar's artistic director Josie Rourke was masterminding the production and she cast Hiddleston in the lead. She had initially approached him with the script, and Tom quickly saw the appeal of doing a play that was not often performed.

'It's challenging – it's political, heated and explosive,' he said.

On the first day of rehearsals Tom came directly from the airport where he'd just landed after taking an overnight flight from Los Angeles. He'd been visiting as part of a whirlwind promotional tour for *Thor: The Dark World*, attending eight premieres in Australia, Korea, China, London, Paris, Berlin, New York and Los Angeles. But there was no time to rest; he had to press on with his next commitment and was keen to get stuck in.

'Tom takes everything he does very, very seriously and works unbelievably hard,' said Rourke of her talented lead.

In preparation for the role, Tom learned the play 'inside out'. 'Words are the key to every role, and for *Coriolanus* they guide the character's voice, manner, and even his heartbeat,' he told *Harper's Bazaar*. 'As I studied the play and became more immersed in it, so many questions arose. Why is he so angry? Why does he hate the people so much?'

The actor had seventy performances to deliver with eight shows per week, so there was a lot of work to be done. 'Mentally, I needed rest because the size and scale of the emotions in a Shakespeare story is always exhausting,' he confessed.

But the role of a war hero also required a great deal of physical preparation: 'I tried to make my body as strong as possible by increasing my physical routine, getting lots of early nights and drinking tons of water.'

In an attempt to really focus on the role he removed himself from any distractions. It was a complicated play and, like every other member of the cast, he wanted to give it his all.

The play involved several fight scenes between Tom and the actor Hadley Fraser. Both men did stunt training with coordinator Richard Ryan. 'On the first day we took it easy on each other, but as it went on we developed a mutual trust and we were able to hit each other harder,' Tom explained. 'You get stronger and your body becomes accustomed to it so it doesn't hurt as much.'

A YouTube promotional video showed Tom preparing

for his role, training for sword fights, getting fit with a skipping rope and having fake wounds applied in Make-up.

'Make-up is crucial because the writing of the play specifically references the bruised, battered and scarred body of Coriolanus,' Tom told *Harper's Bazaar*. 'There's a scene when he refuses to reveal his wounds to the people in the market place, even though that's what's required of him to become a politician.

'Because those injuries are so important, we added a part where Coriolanus has a brief and painful shower and the audience can see the true extent of my wounds.

'To prepare for this my body is covered in paint, latex and stage blood, which takes about an hour to put on. It's so thrilling because when I reveal my body and the wounds, I've heard the audience wince. It's a very important moment because then, when he stands on the senate, the audience believes that he has a right to be there.'

Every day before a 7.30pm performance Tom would arrive at the theatre three hours beforehand. To get in shape for the complex fight scenes, he would have to warm up his body and rehearse sequences. Half an hour before the curtains were up, he'd begin to mentally prepare for the evening's performance.

'Most actors agree that you need to rid yourself of your "day" before you perform, and I've never been able to just walk on stage. You could have an argument with your partner, or you could have been to a birthday party, or whatever. To cleanse yourself of what has gone on before is important; you can't let it affect your performance.'

To get himself in the correct angry frame of mind for the opening scenes, he would sometimes listen to Holst's *The Planets*. And to build up energy he'd run up and down the theatre's fire escape before going on stage.

It would be all too easy to leave the stage bitter and twisted after every show, such were the demands of the character, but Tom found it was fairly straightforward to unwind: 'There is something very satisfying and definite about Coriolanus's death at the end of the play. Everything that he is goes with him.

'Equally, at the end of the play he experiences compassion and it is very therapeutic to be able to finally yield to something soft and vulnerable.'

Taking a long shower to rinse the gory make-up from his body also helped Tom disconnect from the role.

Despite his meticulous preparation there was always scope for making mistakes. During one performance his sword actually snapped in two so he had to carry on with a hand fight. 'It turned out alright in the end though,' laughed Tom after the event. 'Damian Lewis was in the audience and he thought it was on purpose!'

Describing his portrayal of the role to the *Telegraph* newspaper, Hiddleston used the analogy of keys on a piano – 'We have the capacity to experience every aspect of life, don't we? There's love, generosity, hope, kindness, laughter and all the good stuff.

'And then there's grief, hatred, jealousy and pain. The way I see it, life is about trying to get to a place where you feel happy with the chords that you are playing. I'm lucky because I can experiment with all the different notes, via my work.

'And when I hit the right notes, I like to think that I'm conveying some sort of truth.

'That's what, in my dreams, I'm hoping to do with *Coriolanus*; at its absolute best, a play like that can unite its audience. They can go into the theatre as strangers and leave as a group, having understood and been through something important together.

'If I am somehow contributing to that then surely my work is of some consequence.'

A film version of the play was selected for broadcast by London's National Theatre Live and was distributed to cinemas across the UK. 'We had one night, where we went out live to cinemas across the country and across the world!' enthused Tom. 'It was a thrilling thing to be in the very small space in Covent Garden and knowing people were watching you in Boston, Sydney, Sheffield and St Ives. That was very cool.'

He analysed his portrayal of the character in a video which appeared on the National Theatre's website: 'I think in the past audiences have struggled with access to Coriolanus, because he is so hard. He seems impenetrable. But that's the thing that makes him most interesting as a character. He's a man who'd denied himself the most relatable human feelings. He's someone who's vulnerable and impenetrable. He's not someone who's given easily to charm or friendliness or even smiling.'

In many ways Tom admired his character's honesty and his extraordinary physical courage: 'Hamlet is easy to empathise with, Othello has a goodness in him and there is an innate tragedy to watching an old man go mad in *King Lear*. Coriolanus is seen as being unsympathetic and cold, but I actually saw so much vulnerability in him,' he told *Harper's Bazaar*.

The performance was well received by the critics.

'A fast, witty, intelligent production that, in Tom Hiddleston, boasts a fine *Coriolanus*,' wrote the *Guardian*.

'A complex, compelling central performance,' said *Time Out*.

'Tom Hiddleston delivers a powerhouse performance,' praised the *Daily Telegraph*.

The *Observer* also gave it a rapturous reception: 'Tom Hiddleston is the ideal combination of emotional reserve and physical bravura.'

Tom even picked up a Best Actor gong at the 2014 *Evening Standard* Theatre Awards. 'I'm so proud of the production and I'm so proud to represent it here tonight,' he told journalists after the presentation. '*Coriolanus* is a tough play.'

Aside from winning an award, the production genuinely did have a profound impact on Tom. After the final performance he felt compelled to write thank-you notes on copies of the script to every member of the cast and crew.

* * *

Once the run of *Coriolanus* was over, it was time for Tom to return to the world of film. But his latest project couldn't be further removed from the lofty heights of Shakespeare. Next up, he would appear in *Muppets Most Wanted*.

'It's the silliest thing I've ever done!' he exclaimed. But he was attracted by the 'laugh-out-loud' script – it was too good to resist.

It wasn't his first encounter with the popular puppets, though. In 2013, he'd appeared in a viral video with the Cookie Monster. During a break between interviews, he prepares to eat a cookie but is interrupted by the Cookie Monster. Hoping to teach the greedy creature a lesson in delayed gratification, Tom refuses to share the cookie. He then presents him with a plateful of cookies and the Cookie Monster admits it was worth being patient and waiting.

In *Muppets Most Wanted*, Tom had a cameo role as 'the Great Escapo'. A prisoner in Gulag 38B, a prison camp in Siberia, he tries to escape during *The Annual Gulag Revue Show*, but is stopped by Nadya, a feisty prison guard, and her taser.

Promoting the film at the 2014 BAFTA Awards, Tom even sidled up to Miss Piggy on the red carpet to canoodle and give her a kiss. At a premiere of *The Avengers* in Rome, he tweeted a photo of himself and a Kermit doll dressed as Loki.

The movie was yet more evidence of his playful side.

He had also developed a reputation for being quite a mover. Videos of the actor toe-tapping and gyrating his hips had gone viral. 'God, it's so embarrassing!' exclaimed Tom to the *Guardian* in 2016. He insisted the whole thing had started on a chat show in Korea: 'It was a big public Q&A. There were 7,000 people there, and taking questions from the audience. Somebody asked: "Of what body part are you most proud?" That's just a wrong question, to which there are only wrong answers. So I said, "My feet."' When asked why, he replied: 'Without my feet, I couldn't run and I couldn't dance.' Then they asked him to demonstrate his skills and he dutifully obliged – 'So I danced... And I created a monster.'

* * *

The last twelve months had been relentless so having some free time allowed Tom to catch up with friends and family. In July 2013 he was spotted watching Andy Murray play at Wimbledon with record executive Jane Arthy, fuelling rumours they might be an item. But he was quick to dispel any gossip.

'I understand the curiosity,' he told the press. 'One day I hope when there's really something to write home about, then I'll be able to talk.'

Following his cameo in *Muppets Most Wanted*, Tom's next cinema appearance was in the animation *Tinker Bell and The Pirate Fairy* (2014). Here, he would provide the voice of Captain Hook.

The swashbuckling plot followed the misadventures of fairy Zarina (Christina Hendricks), who flees Pixie Hollow and joins forces with the pirates of Skull Rock, led by a cabin boy who later becomes Captain Hook. Tinker Bell (Mae Whitman) goes in search of her friend and a battle commences.

Tom had always been a fan of Peter Pan and had grown up reading J.M. Barrie's book. He and his sisters would watch the Disney film version again and again but he could never have imagined he'd end up starring in a version of the film. He was extremely proud to have been offered the role. When the script landed on his desk and he was invited to audition, he thought it was 'a no-brainer'.

'I always wanted to play a Disney animation character and for it to be Captain Hook,' he told the website *Hitthefloor*.

Although he didn't actually appear on screen, the role was demanding in many other ways. It required him to make his debut singing performance. 'I've done books on tape and commercial voice work – but singing in a studio was completely new to me,' he told *Hitthefloor* in an interview. 'I've sung on stage and I've been in musicals but singing in a studio was a real thrill.'

Tom had grown up listening to Disney musicals such as *The Lion King* and *The Jungle Book*, so he relished the opportunity to have a go at it himself. 'I was a bit scared at first,' he confessed. 'After warming up, I had the time of my life in there. I found my voice and it was great. It was really fun.'

Using only his voice to act was also a challenge: 'You're stripped of your body and you're stripped of your eyes, which tell so much story when you're doing live-action work,' he explained.

Admittedly he had to work harder, but the reward was having a 'freer rein because the only ceiling on the work is your imagination'. He also looked forward to seeing the reaction of his niece, who was a big fan of *Peter Pan*: 'One day, when I have kids of my own, I hope they'll see it, too. I hope they laugh about their dad playing this iconic role.'

Appropriately rounding off his year of cutesiness, Tom posted a 39-second video to YouTube, which featured him singing 'We Wish You a Merry Christmas' while holding a puppy on his lap. As he strummed away on his guitar, he looked devilishly handsome. The video was posted by Joanne Gardner, who said the footage was filmed in country singer Rodney Crowell's Nashville studio 'during a short break' as he and Hiddleston worked on the soundtrack for the Hank Williams' biopic *I Saw the Light*, one of Tom's next big films.

For many, it was the perfect Christmas gift.

CHAPTER TWELVE

A GOTHIC ROMANCE

After a brief break away from the big screen, 2015 was set to be a significant year for Tom. He would feature in three major film releases.

The first big project was the Gothic horror movie *Crimson Peak*, helmed by Mexican director Guillermo del Toro. Hiddleston recalled receiving a phone call asking him if he'd be interested in playing the role of Thomas Sharpe, a baronet who turns out to be a murderer.

'It happened very fast, actually,' revealed Tom to website *Fangoria*. 'I was in Los Angeles in August 2013, and I got a phone call from my agent connecting me to Guillermo del Toro.

'He said he was going to rewrite this role in *Crimson Peak* for me, and he was going to send it to me the next day. And then, suddenly, I got an e-mail from Jessica Chastain, who's been a friend of mine for a while, saying, "I really want you to do Crimson," and I said, "Yeah, yeah, yeah, OK, OK! Guillermo just wants me to read it first." So he sent it to me, I read it and loved it, and I flew to Toronto the next day. We had breakfast, and by the time we got to lunchtime I said yes, and we were off.'

Over breakfast, the pair discussed 'Gothic romance and tall, dark strangers and innocent, pure-hearted heroines'. 'We talked about Rochester in *Jane Eyre*, we talked about Bluebeard, and his idea of the Byronic hero,' Tom told the *Wall Street Journal*. 'There were archetypes we needed to present, to create expectations which we could subvert and confound.'

Then del Toro drove him over to Pinewood Toronto Studios.

'He introduced me to Tom Sanders and Kate Hawley, the production designer and costume designer, and Tom had already built the set in miniature. So I was able to go back to London with an idea in my mind of what the world was going to be like. And Kate had already put together a whole wall of visual inspiration, with paintings and photographs, stuff from the period, high fashion, images of the landscape of the north of England in the late 19th century; it was truly inspiring. I went back with a head full of images.'

Tom's friend Benedict Cumberbatch had originally been earmarked for the role, but when he pulled out, Hiddleston seemed an ideal choice.

'I don't know why he dropped out, but he did, and it

meant that Guillermo had to find someone to play the role and he came to me,' recalled Tom.

He was excited to receive the call from del Toro, a director whose work he'd always admired, and wasn't at all precious about being second choice. The film sounded like an interesting project and he was immediately drawn to the complexities of his character.

'I'm fascinated by characters like that,' he said. 'Because it's so universal. We put our best foot forward, we're optimistic and engaging but that often masks a more turbulent private life. I think that's true of everyone that I've ever met.

'It's what makes people interesting, that tension. We're all frail, as Angelo says in *Measure for Measure*. We are all consistently inconsistent.'

Del Toro even went on to tweak the role and adapt it specifically for Hiddleston – 'He rewrote the role a little bit, to make it more custom-made for me in some way, which is amazing of him.'

The director also presented Tom with a short biography of his character's backstory so he could really get a feel for the part.

'Guillermo and I were always trying to find the subtlety and the precision of that very complex psychology,' Tom told the *Wall Street Journal*. 'He's [Thomas] very trapped, struggling to free himself from the bonds of the past.'

Del Toro had approached him for the role because he believed he was exactly the right actor who could portray

Thomas Sharpe's inner conflict. 'I wanted a guy who would have humanity, and would understand that the crux of the love story is not to expiate any guilt,' he told the *Wall Street Journal*. 'I wanted him to be guilty of all charges, but wanted us to share his journey of developing a soul and a conscience.'

He had first noticed Tom's acting skills in *Wallander*, the BBC TV series in which he starred with Kenneth Branagh. 'It was a small role, but he had a very striking, doomed look,' said del Toro. 'I took a little mental note. Then when I saw him as Loki, he made me understand the internal struggle of that character in a pulp narrative.'

In a similar vein to del Toro's previous films, *The Devil's Backbone* and *Pan's Labyrinth*, this would be a spine-chilling and visually opulent piece of cinema. The plot was dark, twisted and imaginative.

Seeking investment for his new invention, a machine to mine clay, Thomas Sharpe leaves his mansion in Victorian England and, accompanied by his sister, Lady Lucille Sharpe (played by Tom's long-time friend Jessica Chastain), heads to America. There, he falls in love with Edith Cushing (Mia Wasikowska), an author haunted by the death of her mother. They marry and return to England, where nightmarish visions lead Edith to discover even darker truths.

'It's the biggest set I've ever been on in my life. It has demons and secrets the same way a human being does,' explained Tom. 'Thomas Sharpe has a very old house, with a lot of dark secrets. And he would love to [escape]. He has a compulsion to live in the future, to create. He's an inventor, an engineer. He wants to make things. But his inheritance is very complex. His physical inheritance is this dilapidated mansion, which has lots of dark secrets. And his emotional and psychological inheritance that weighs very heavily on his soul.

'It's a Gothic romance, and it's true to Gothic romance in that there's a beautiful, radiant heroine played by Mia, who is sensational, and she's drawn to the tall, dark stranger with the crumbling mansion on the hill,' he told chat show host Graham Norton.

'It's sort of like she's Elizabeth Bennet and I'm Mr Darcy, but when she gets back to the house, it's full of crazy shit.

'It's about these polar opposites of sex and death, these two completely opposite forces in our lives.'

Along with a fascination for the script, Hiddleston was also attracted by the prospect of working with Guillermo del Toro, whom he described as 'a master'. 'Guillermo is probably, if not definitely, the primary interpreter of Gothic romance in contemporary cinema,' he gushed. 'He has the capacity to make stories about the supernatural intensely emotional and accessible.'

'This felt like new territory for me,' Tom told the website *Collider*. 'In Greco-Roman drama there are specific archetypes; in this film it's a battle between something that's pre-determined and taking control of your life.

'Shakespeare and Chekhov write about dynasties. Gothic

romance has its own place and particular flavour. This felt quite new for me, which I found thrilling.'

* * *

Once again, as with his previous films Tom climbed inside the mind of his character easily: 'There is a part of his charisma that's performed and presented, and there's a part of his charisma that's very genuine. His enthusiasm about the future is very real and he has an innate gift. Perhaps he is used to people buying what he's selling.

'I tried to build a character with lots of layers; he was someone who had a lot of private pain. He feels guilty about so much. What you see is charm, behind that is guilt and behind that is vulnerability.'

Del Toro certainly had some very unconventional working methods. The director even made a full body cast of Hiddleston in preparation for the film.

'I think with Guillermo's films, he makes a full-body cast of everyone,' laughed Tom to reporters. 'I think it's DDT, they're an incredible special effects makeup company. I think it's just that Guillermo started in Makeup, and anything he can do for that, he does. So we have the option.'

Shortly before filming was due to commence, Guillermo del Toro and Jessica Chastain flew to London to see Tom. At the time he was performing on stage in *Coriolanus*. 'We spent a Sunday. Just sat around a table being incredibly precise about the damage done to Thomas and Lucille Sharpe as children,' Tom explained: 'Even though they sometimes are terrifying and formidable, we at least have compassion for their predicament.'

He also relished the opportunity to sink his teeth into the Gothic romance genre. As a teen, he'd read several books in a similar vein.

'It's interesting; I believe those archetypes and characters still feature in our imaginations in a way we're almost not aware of. You think about musical lyrics, and people still talk about tall, dark strangers and the mystery and allure of a certain type of man or woman, if that makes sense. The Gothic style is imbued with a particular type of sexuality that people are still invested in.'

The film featured some extremely terrifying scenes, and Tom admitted to the *Irish Examiner* that he was a bit of a coward when it came to horror movies: 'I've always enjoyed ghost stories but I'm not great with horror myself, as an audience member,' he confessed. At school, though, he'd been a big fan of ghost stories in literature. He'd been lucky enough to have decent English teachers who'd really helped to open his imagination to the genre.

One of his favourite tutors would always read M.R. James books aloud, because he 'knew none of us were going to pay attention on a Friday afternoon, because we were all thinking about cake and conkers and running about'. As a result, Tom had made a 'powerful' connection with the English author and medievalist scholar, who was regarded as the originator of the 'antiquarian ghost story' and considered one of the best in the genre.

'It's something I've never forgotten,' said Tom.

So did he believe in ghosts now, asked one reporter during promotion for the film.

'I believe in *Ghostbusters*, and therefore if we have to have ghosts in order to get to *Ghostbusters*, then I'm happy,' he said, before quickly adding, 'Sorry, I'm being flippant. I have had weird experiences actually, but I do think they're projections of my own imagination. So I do wake up and I'm creeped out, I turn my light on and look under the bed. But then the next morning, you tell the story over breakfast and you go, "I'm such an idiot", something's going on up here [he taps his head], rather than anything else.

'My imagination wants to believe in ghosts,' he went on. 'I certainly loved ghosts as a child. I'm sure there are people who could explain the physical impossibility of supernatural phenomena, but it's more fun to believe in a world with ghosts – if only because it's fun to believe in a world with *Ghostbusters*.'

Still, he did confess to occasionally having 'terrifying' nightmares about the 'profoundly disturbing' Child Catcher in the film *Chitty Chitty Bang Bang*.

Director Guillermo del Toro, however, firmly declared he believed in ghosts.

'I have experienced [ghosts] and I believe,' he told MTV. 'Everybody in my family, most people have experienced that. I don't know if it's in the water but in Mexico, it's more usual to encounter the strange and the supernatural.'

In the same interview Jessica Chastain admitted she

believed in both ghosts and aliens, but Mia Wasikowska said that although she felt metaphorical ghosts have power, the real danger is humans.

Thanks to an excellent make-up team, the actual ghosts in the film appeared to be frighteningly realistic. 'I wasn't in many of the scenes with the ghosts, but I did see them in costume and in makeup, and it was kind of extraordinary,' said Tom to the *Fangoria* website in 2015. 'It was like seeing a creature from the wild – an astonishing thing to be in the presence of. The makeup artists, David Martí and Montse Ribé, who also did the creatures for *Pan's Labyrinth*, are first-rate practitioners of their craft.'

The production efforts for *Crimson Peak* were indeed impressive. Tom fell in love with the set: 'Honestly, it was just breathtaking. It was so beautiful and completely realized. Often, as an actor, you're asked to supply the details of a scene in your imagination, but there was no extra work required here. We were all actually in the house; all we had to do was turn up and be there.'

* * *

Despite the dark nature of the film, Tom never felt gloomy or melancholic on set. That's part of the discipline of being an actor – to keep the intensity of the experience at work and not take it home otherwise it can be quite dangerous and damaging. 'There were some intense days, but mercifully, I wasn't staying in Crimson Peak myself, I was staying in a nice hotel where I could get a hamburger and a cold beer,' he joked.

His co-star, Jessica Chastain, would cover the walls of her trailer with pictures of serial killers to help get to grips with the horror of the film; Tom chose to look at mood boards created by costume designer Kate Hawley.

'There was one painting by Caspar David Friedrich called *Wanderer Above the Sea of Fog*, which is very powerful. It's the back of a gentleman standing on a rock in the middle of a storm. It channels the passion of the romantics,' he told the *Plymouth Herald* in 2015.

The horror scenes were certainly striking, but one of the most memorable moments in the film involved a scene in which Tom bared his all, stripping off in front of the cameras. Needless to say, fans revelled in the footage.

'Guillermo was like, "Dude, it's time to get naked, man. You have to show the world your buns",' joked Tom on *The Graham Norton Show*.

But on the American chat show *The Late Show* with Stephen Colbert, del Toro pointed out that it was actually all Hiddleston's doing.

'He likes to say it was my idea,' Guillermo said, 'but it was totally his idea.'

In actual fact, Tom had actively lobbied for the scenes. But his desire to expose flesh had nothing to do with showing off, he genuinely believed the scenes would heighten the power of the film, which he believed wavered on a thin line between sex and violence. He also thought it was unfair that female actors often had to appear naked; perhaps it was time to even things out.

'I didn't have a problem with the nakedness because there's always been a strain of sexuality in Gothic romance as much as there has been about the fear of death and the threat of violence. It's a very violent film and I felt we needed to balance that. If we were going to bring up the violence, we needed to bring up the sense of sexuality as well.

'I was happy to do it,' he insisted. 'It's so often in movies that women are more naked than men, and I think that's unfair. We wanted to redress the balance. It was really important for us that Edith was calling the shots, that she's the strongest character. She's a strong woman and she calls the shots.'

Tom wasn't embarrassed about showing off his body, even though he was far from being an exhibitionist. 'If it's part of the story and it's intrinsic to it, I don't have any vanity about that, specifically with *Crimson Peak*,' he told MTV. 'It's a Gothic romance, and underneath a Gothic romance are these polarizing forces of sex and death.

'I realized that scene in *Crimson Peak* is such a huge and profound part of the story,' he added. 'That's where the love story begins, and it comes out of a sexuality, so I was kind of okay with that.'

The film was steeped in sensuality and in 2015 website *Bustle* even compiled their Top 10 of Tom's most sexy moments: 'There are plenty of sexy Tom Hiddleston moments in *Crimson Peak*,' they wrote, 'and fans everywhere will be thrilled.

'It's hard to pinpoint exactly what the best Hiddleston

scene in *Crimson Peak* truly is, as there are so very many to choose from. Is it when he, as the mysterious Brit Thomas Sharpe, shows up uninvited to Edith's home to take her to a dance? Or when he looks her dead in the eyes and asks, "Would you be mine?" Or is it when he disrobes on a cold winter's night to have sex with his wife for the first time? So many choices!

'If director Guillermo del Toro was hoping to make a film that would inspire countless Hiddlestoners to explode with lust, he just might have succeeded with *Crimson Peak*.'

Along with the romance between Edith and Thomas, there were also hints of a strong bond between the protagonist and his sister Lucille. 'The thing about Gothic romance is there's always a sexuality at play. And incest has been something that's been hinted at by other novels in the genre,' Tom told the website *io9*.

'It's an interesting dynamic. They're a brother and a sister who've been orphaned, and they're in this big old house, and they have a very deep connection. But there's a lot of other romantic elements in the film, too.

'The idea that your sexuality impels you into situations that may be dangerous; it always happens to the heroine. She's drawn by the magnetism of a tall, dark stranger, and suddenly she's in an insecure place. The inversion is that through Edith, Thomas experiences a healthy sexuality for the very first time and that changes who he becomes.'

Tom had known Jessica Chastain (who played his sister Lucille) for several years and revealed, 'it was nice to go into that sibling partnership knowing each other from before.' There were even rumours the two actors were dating. Gossip pages suggested Jessica had even been to visit Tom's parents.

'Tom is taken with Jess and it's serious,' a source told *Glamour* magazine. 'Before Christmas she visited Britain to stay with him and meet all his family for the first time.'

But the actress, who won a Golden Globe in 2013 for her role as a CIA agent in Kathryn Bigelow's film *Zero Dark Thirty*, had already told the press she had a 'no actor' policy when it came to romance. She once revealed: 'In this business it's very tough to maintain a relationship because we're like gypsies – always on the move. And the more you share your relationship with the world, the less special it becomes. So I always try to keep my dating life quiet.'

Tom had also had previous experience of working with his other leading lady, Mia Wasikowska, on the Jim Jarmusch film *Only Lovers Left Alive* (2013). It had been another dark and macabre film, in which he and Tilda Swinton had both played vampires. Wasikowska had played the character of Ava, Tilda Swinton's younger sister.

Tom told *Esquire* in 2016 'My character in the film, in his house in Detroit, has this wall of fame on which he hung portraits of people he thought contributed most significantly to the evolution of genetics. Christopher Marlowe is on the wall, and Isaac Newton, and Nikola Tesla and Iggy Pop and Rodney Dangerfield. It's a witty gallery of heroes.'

But by the time filming wrapped on *Crimson Peak*, Tom was ready to move on to more light-hearted material: 'I need to see the sunshine,' he told friends, 'and I need to swim in the ocean, and I need to be my blond self for a bit.'

Shooting some scenes had been extremely demanding.

'There was one scene in particular that was very difficult for me to film. And my character was emotional. There's a sequence in the film that goes on forever and it's physically draining and emotionally draining,' he told *Gizmodo* in 2015. 'I hope at some point to see some behind-the-scenes pics of all of us in the scene. Because I imagine when we weren't filming, we were just like... urgh. I was covered in bruises, and that was tough.'

He had amassed a huge amount of respect for Guillermo del Toro: 'He's able to blend what we see with what we dream and make it seem like it's part of the same fabric. That's very inspiring...

'The thing about Guillermo that is less remarked on is his sensitivity and his sincerity. He's incredibly sincere as a filmmaker. If you think about *The Devil's Backbone*, *Pan's Labyrinth*, and *Crimson Peak* – and I do think that those three films fit together in his own mind and are very similar in their tone – there is a childlike innocence or open-heartedness. Guillermo is never glib or cynical or ironic. Everything is fully invested with meaning.

'But I was ready to leave the world of *Crimson Peak* by the time we finished. Thomas Sharpe is a very dark character in many respects.'

Despite being given an R rating for bloody violence, some sexual content and brief strong language, *Crimson Peak* was well received by critics.

'Guillermo del Toro returns to his roots with a sumptuous horror steeped in 19th-century fiction and classic cinema,' wrote Mark Kermode in the *Guardian*.

'Even the pristine white snow bleeds bright scarlet in *Crimson Peak*, the malformed love child between a richly atmospheric gothic romance and an overripe Italian giallo,' said Peter Debruge for *Variety*.

But the *Telegraph* newspaper even went so far as to call it 'voluptuously horrible', giving it four stars out of five: 'Del Toro's ninth feature is a swooning, swirling Victorian romance splattered with the bright blood of classic Hammer horror: in short, think Du Maurier, but gorier,' wrote Robbie Collin. 'The film seems to be perpetually teetering on the brink of breathless climax.'

Sadly, the film didn't perform particularly well at the box office, though.

Tom shrugged off the lacklustre figures. He'd had his fair share of blockbusters, and doing this film had never been about earning big bucks. It had been about earning recognition, and given the praise heaped upon him for his portrayal of the charming and seductive Sir Thomas Sharpe, he'd certainly been successful in fulfilling his ambitions.

CHAPTER THIRTEEN

HIGH-RISE

Tom's next project seemed just as outlandish as *Crimson Peak* – in fact, it was even more so. *High-Rise* (2015), directed by Ben Wheatley, was an adaptation of J.G. Ballard's classic 1975 thriller. The stellar line-up would include Jeremy Irons, Sienna Miller, Luke Evans and Elisabeth Moss.

At the time of writing, Ballard had claimed his novel was set 'five minutes in the future'. It was his dystopian vision of the future and a warning for what might lie ahead.

'Ballard said he saw himself as a man standing at the side of the road with a sign saying "Caution, bends ahead!"' Tom told *Time Out* magazine in 2016.

'*High-Rise* was inspired by a holiday he took in Spain. Ballard was staying in a block of flats and tourists would have these tremendous arguments about territory. "You can't drop your cigarette butts on my balcony!" "This is my swimming pool!" Everyone had a perfect view of the Mediterranean, life was beautiful, and yet British holidaymakers would fight about things. Everyone would sweat the small stuff.'

The story looks at the decline of the building as its technology and services start to break down. Each floor represents a different class within society. Mirroring the downfall of the building, residents also let rip, indulging in wild parties, sex and riots to reach the top floor.

The film stars Jeremy Irons as Royal, an architect living on the top floor of the block with his wife Ann, played by Keeley Hawes, who would often parade around their grand folly of a rooftop garden dressed as Little Bo Peep.

Director Ben Wheatley interpreted the book's title as being more than just about a block of flats: 'It's a metaphor. It's a building; it's also a man or a woman. It's a country; it's the world. It works on all those different levels,' he revealed to the *Telegraph*.

'The reason we wanted to adapt *High-Rise* is because it felt to us like it had come of age. Reading it, it felt more like the pages of a newspaper than a novel.

'The thing that struck me most when I re-read it was the way that the people in the tower would film everything on Super-8 cameras, and project it back to share with everyone in the building. It felt very much like social media.'

Tom agreed with his director. He'd always been fascinated by the author J.G. Ballard and thought he was in many ways a genius. 'My first introduction came when I was at college and my best friend at the time was a huge fan,' he told *The New York Times*. 'He was reading *Concrete Island* and *Cocaine Nights*. He was always very vocal about Ballard's prescience. As a science-fiction writer, Ballard saw where the world was going. He was fascinated by technology and our obsession with it. *High-Rise* was written in 1975, but if you read it, it feels like today.

'"The building is a diseased body,"' he continued, quoting lines from the book. '"The lights are like neurons in a brain, the elevators are like pistons in the chambers of the heart." He was so prescient, Ballard. The book talks about how the residents shoot these orgiastic parties and project them against the wall for their neighbours. And that's the beginning of social media. He saw it all coming.'

'I think it's no coincidence that he's called Royal,' said Jeremy Irons of his character in an interview with the *Telegraph* in 2016. 'He's interested in how best we can organise society. He hoped the building would be "a crucible for change" in people's lives – and it certainly is that, but not as he expected.'

Hiddleston was cast in the role of physiologist Robert Laing, who occupies an apartment on the twenty-fifth floor. He was one of the first actors to sign up.

'I read the script and it was sensational,' he gushed to the *Telegraph* in 2016. 'It was clear and funny and dark and true.

'I could see that in its DNA, it was political, and it was

time to turn my face to the wind of that,' he added. 'I'm inspired by something Alan Rickman said: "if you want to know who I am, it's all in the work".'

He first got involved with the project through producer Jeremy Thomas, who had also worked with him on the film *Only Lovers Left Alive*. 'He'd been trying to get this made for a long time,' recalled Tom. 'The combination of Jeremy with director Ben Wheatley, and the material of author J.G. Ballard was a thrilling proposition.'

He described Wheatley as a 'very singular voice in British cinema'. The director, in turn, was also very keen to work with Hiddleston. He'd seen him in *The Avengers* and thought he was 'brilliant'.

'That film should be called "Loki,"' he said at the time. 'They're really just supporting characters in the story of this disaffected madman trying to please his father.'

Bizarrely, when Wheatley and his wife Amy Jump (the film's screenwriter) were making the movie, they had a picture of Tom Hiddleston stuck to their fridge. Tom said he found the idea 'initially disconcerting' but then understood it as a 'huge compliment'.

Sienna Miller was also cast in the film. She played Charlotte, a neighbour to Tom's character. 'She's a selfish and kind of interesting woman,' said the actress of her role in an interview with *Paper*. 'She falls into the middle-class category, but it's quite mercurial and she manages to move seamlessly between the upper and lower floors.'

Miller admitted this was 'probably the most experimental

and dark film I've ever done.' She was desperate to do a film with Ben Wheatley and admitted she'd even have been happy 'doing the tea on Ben's set'.

'There was no "too far" with this film,' she added. 'We got to push our boundaries.'

For the most part Tom's character, Robert, is an observer: 'The most fascinating thing for me was that Laing is reactive, whereas other people are proactive. He's quiet and watchful, while the other inhabitants are sliding into a kind of chaos,' the actor told *Esquire* in 2016.

'Because of his profession as a physiologist I think he has a kind of intellectual detachment about disease and human impulses, so he's able to withdraw emotionally from the psychological impact of this feral chaos.'

But events in the building begin to impact on Robert's mental health.

'He wants this blank, fresh, new, clean, modern start in the high rise. The impact of the building on his mind creates a volatility in him that's very visible and dark,' added Tom of his character, who initially appears on screen in a grey suit inspired by George Lazenby's look in the 1969 Bond movie, *On Her Majesty's Secret Service*.

'Tom seems to have that aura – tall, slim and elegant,' revealed costume designer Odile Dicks-Mireaux to the *Telegraph* in 2016. 'He was hesitant about the longer jacket and wider lapels, but it's totally a 1970s suit. Yet it has a narrow tie, which has to do with Laing feeling constricted.'

As the film progresses, Robert's smart demeanour

diminishes: 'There's a key scene when he walks out of his flat in a clean shirt, then thinks again, goes back inside and changes into a dirty one – which he feels better represents who he is becoming. It's a sort of breakdown, I suppose,' Hiddleston told the *Telegraph* in 2016.

In one scene, Tom even loses his clothes altogether. Lying naked on a sun lounger, arms folded behind his head, he has just a magazine to protect his modesty. The shot would become an internet sensation, still circulating on social media today, but Hiddleston was quick to point out that it was in no way gratuitous.

'Nudity has always been part of the story and it's never felt gratuitous. It's always felt as if it's in service of something,' he told the website *Complex*. 'In *High-Rise*, it's quite symbolic. Laing moves into the building to get away from the entanglements of real life. And the first thing he does in this new, clean, clinical space is take all his clothes off and sunbathe. And within seconds, that peace and freedom is interrupted. And then he never takes his clothes off again. And that's in the novel. I felt it was kind of important, and honestly, you don't see anything more than you would see if I was just walking down the beach, so I didn't have a problem with it.'

His co-star Sienna Miller agreed. 'No-one really likes doing nudity,' she laughed. 'But Tom's very professional, and if the script calls for it, he'll get his Hiddlebum out!'

Tom agreed with *Time Out* magazine that the plot had a definite political edge: 'Some people might see it as a

Lord of the Flies-type experiment of stripping away the mask of civil manners to reveal the animal underneath – and it just happens to be located in a British building in the 1970s with adults as opposed to children on a desert island.'

He pointed out that parallels could easily be drawn with contemporary society, where power lay in the hands of a very small group of privileged people.

'It's a very obvious metaphor,' he told *Esquire*. 'There's unequal access to the resources in the building, depending on where you live. The people on the lower floors are furious that in the penthouse they still have electricity [while] the lights go out in the basement, or that the swimming pool is closed to children from the lower floors.

'There's a righteous moral anger about inequality that's being told there. And perhaps Ballard is saying that it's inevitable. He's saying that it's part of the human condition, some sort of striving for status.'

He had closely re-read Ballard's book to delve into the mind of his character: 'I took my cue from the book, and I found it fascinating that J.G. Ballard chooses his leading character to be a physiologist, someone who understands the mechanical engineering of the human brain and body.

'I found that he's a character who has a lot of private guilt and shame. He's moved into this building to get away from the complexities of life. He's trying to stay detached, and he actually can't. It's all about his unprocessed guilt. There's a lot of guilt going around, he's trying to get away from real life. He wants to live in a grey flat and wear a grey suit and not be affected.'

Eager, as ever, to give 100 per cent to his role, Tom thought it would be a good idea to study the working day of a physiologist. He contacted a forensic pathologist in Nottingham and asked if he could come along to watch him perform an autopsy.

'I wanted to understand the perspective of the people who do that every day, who have a sensitivity to that kind of work but also have the scientific rigor,' he told *Esquire*. 'They can actually deconstruct a body and [determine] the cause of death. These are the people we depend on in our society, and if someone falls dead in the middle of the street, the forensic pathologist will cut them open and tell us why.'

The body he witnessed being dissected belonged to a young boxer who'd died in the ring.

'I watched them cut a man open,' he recalled. 'It was a very, very tough experience...

'I couldn't handle it. What overwhelmed me was the smell. I had to go outside and vomit. Then I went back in and found it fascinating to see the engineering of the human body. But you need a strong stomach for that stuff.'

It verged on being a harrowing experience, but Tom believed it was very much necessary to really understand his role: 'If you have to perform something on camera, you want to make sure people who actually do that go, "Yeah, that's how you do that,"' he told the website *Business*

Insider. 'The reason I went to the autopsy was there was no one I knew who had the authority of how to do this. I didn't have the first clue.'

Plus, it set him up to deal with the more squeamish scenes, such as tearing flesh from a skull: 'I think that scene's a declaration of intent by Ben [Wheatley]. You see Dr Laing peeling the facial tissue off her head to reveal the blood and the bones beneath. I think that's sort of what Ballard is doing to society. He's saying, "Let me take away the surface and show you the flesh and blood beneath."'

To prepare for the part, Tom also invested a great deal of time in trying to understand exactly what the director wanted from the film.

'I wanted to sync up with Ben,' he told *Esquire*. 'I always do that when I sign on to a film: I try to sync up with the tone of what a director is trying to do.

'I ask them to give me some movies to watch, give me some books to read, give me some music to listen to – to try and find a framework they are working in so I can place myself within it.

'I love Ben's work. He's rebellious and he's mischievous and has his own singular sense of humour and taste.'

Filming took place at an accelerating pace.

'I think on the first day we got through 32 set-ups,' Tom told the *Telegraph*. 'You're just gunning through it; there's a great momentum. You don't have time to get complacent – you're on your toes all the time. Ben is so easy and good-natured, but you finish the day and you have this extraordinary amount of footage. It's been astonishing.'

* * *

Several scenes were shot at the late nineteenth-century, ground-level Bangor Castle Walled Garden, just outside Belfast. But thanks to digital wizardry, it would appear as a rooftop garden forty storeys high. The production team also made use of a nearby derelict leisure centre to provide an apt setting for the breakdown in order that occurs in the film.

During the shoot, Tom became good friends with many of the actors and the production team, telling *Business Insider* in 2016: 'We all became very close, which was nice. We all stayed in the same hotel for six or seven weeks. But I found it very reassuring that we were in Northern Ireland in a seaside town where you can get fish and chips all the time.

'The set was a contained madhouse. But we were shooting from 8 a.m. to 6 p.m. every day and we would emerge into the evening covered in all kinds of stuff going. We would go have a shower and meet for fish and chips. That was actually quite healthy.'

Onscreen, many of the party scenes were actually very enjoyable to film: 'The parties were so fun because we would set them up and, of course, there's no real alcohol, but there is real music and Ben would put on music and we'd start dancing.

'The camera would stay rolling, and he would say, "Crazy, go crazy, dance more crazy, more crazy dancing."

He would gently encourage everybody to get a little more wild, but there was something very safe about it.'

One of his favourite scenes involved a dream dance sequence with several air stewards. 'It actually was my idea,' he recalled proudly, explaining the sequence of events to journalists. 'But it wasn't my idea to dance. We shot it at the end of our first day. We were due to wrap at 6 p.m. and at 5:45 they started doing that scene.

'These flight attendants were walking down the corridor and I was watching it and I said to Ben, "Do you think that Laing should be a participant in his own dream?" And he said, "Well, yeah, it'd be nice to have the option." I asked, "What do you think he should be doing? Is he walking in front of them or behind them?" And then he said, "He should be dancing with them." So we did it, and we did it once. We put on Sister Sledge's "Lost in Music" and we danced down the corridor. It was great.'

'We had the best time,' cooed Sienna Miller. 'It's such a crazy, off-the wall story and we were a really close group. We all had dinner together every night and we all took over the bar!

'It was like a proper British independent film and I cannot wait to see everyone!'

* * *

Once filming wrapped, Tom presented cast and crew with a mug and a note to thank them for their efforts on the film. Everyone agreed he was a great guy.

'There are a lot of things about Tom!' co-star Lee Evans told *Nylon* magazine. 'His charm, his charisma, he's a really lovely man. He's very fun. On the film set, he works incredibly hard. He's very committed to the work that he does, and it's enjoyable to work with somebody like that.'

'He's also iconic to super fans because of the roles he's played,' added Sienna Miller. 'The fans of those Marvel films are just another level, another creed. He has a sort of intelligence and wit and looks and charm to back it up.'

When the movie finally hit cinemas, Tom already knew it was likely to garner a mixed response.

'One never knows what will resonate with an audience,' said Jeremy Irons to the *Telegraph* in 2016. 'But I think it's going to look extraordinary. I can't think of another film like it.'

In fact the film divided critics. *The Week* referred to it as the ultimate 'marmite' film. Some had drawn comparisons with *The Lord of the Flies* and *A Clockwork Orange*.

Scarlett Russell at *Digital Spy* said the apocalypse 'never looked prettier', adding: 'Political themes of class war and poverty are peppered with humour, while scenes of violence and even rape are softened by stunningly psychedelic photography.'

The *Guardian*'s Peter Bradshaw also praised the movie for its 'gnomic refusal of normal storytelling and the way it approximates the distance of Ballard's prose'. He even called it 'the social-surrealist film of the year'.

But others criticised the violence and misogyny.

'Wheatley is so in love with his own visual style and excesses that all allegory and satire is lost while the violence escalates and women are beaten then raped,' wrote Deborah Ross at *The Spectator*. 'Misogyny with social commentary comments on misogyny, but without that it's just misogyny served up for its entertainment value.'

Nigel Andrews of the *Financial Times* was even more damning, giving *High-Rise* just one star: 'The film begins with a dog's dinner and then becomes one.'

Such wildly varied reviews were exactly what cast and crew had expected.

'It's provocative, and deliberately so,' said Hiddleston. 'I'm aware that it's like hot mustard in that it has divided people [at the Toronto and London film festivals], but the book opens with the line: "Later, as he sat on his balcony eating the dog, Dr Robert Laing reflected on the unusual events that had taken place within this huge apartment building during the previous three months." Some people are shocked by that.

'But I think the film is true to Ballard, and at the same time a Ben Wheatley film. It has a very British sense of humour, with a uniquely British underbelly of dark, troubling material, which is absolutely part of the history of our culture and our filmmaking. Ben's directing heroes are Lindsay Anderson and Stanley Kubrick and Ken Russell. There is a mischief in his work, a visual and thematic rebellion.'

Some people even walked out of the cinema when

the film was screened at the Toronto Film Festival in September 2015.

'It can be bruising on the day, but it's fine,' Ben Wheatley told *Variety*. 'I get worried that one day you'll make a film nobody will go and see. But at least people are passionate about it.'

Besides, he pointed out the reception to the 'dog' scene could have been worse: 'Even in the U.K., which is internationally famous as a place for dog lovers, there hasn't been much [outrage]. We thought it would be massively controversial. Not that we were courting it, we didn't put it in on purpose. It was in the book.'

But Tom took the reviews in his stride. He'd always known the film would be controversial, but it had allowed him to develop and grow as an actor. It was roles such as this, after all, that would help shape his career. He used the analogy of travel as a way to explain his continuing desire to stretch his abilities by signing up to challenging projects.

'When you're born, you get used to your cot and your crib. And then you get used to your bedroom. Then you get used to your family home, and your school and your town. And then eventually you want to get out of that – you want to broaden your horizons, and the process of being an actor is that. I feel like I want to travel far and wide, and that's why I choose to do different projects. I don't know where the confidence comes from. I think it comes more from curiosity than confidence'.

CHAPTER FOURTEEN

A LABOUR
OF LOVE

Tom didn't have long to sit around and dwell on the critical response to *High-Rise*. He was already well underway with his next project, *I Saw the Light* (2015), a biopic of the country-western star Hank Williams. He'd had literally a week's break between shooting the two films back to back. It was a miracle he managed to remain so upbeat and smiley when anyone else would have been left ragged by such a punishing schedule.

'It was very strange,' he said. 'I'm happy I had the week off. I finished *High-Rise* on the 25th of August 2014, and I landed in Nashville on the 2nd of September.

'I think it took me a while to shake *High-Rise*, in a way. When you've been immersed in one particular environment, it casts a shadow for a time. It was mad, thinking about it. Thank God I went straight to Tennessee, because otherwise I would never have been able to get my head in the game.'

He was cast in the lead role of the Alabamian singer who revolutionised country music following the end of World War II. The story would cover his rise to fame and his difficult relationship with his wife, Audrey, as well as his struggles with substance abuse and spina bifida occulta. Eventually he would die on New Year's Day 1953.

For many, Hiddleston was an outside choice for the role. The actor was four years older than the singer at the time of his death and his upper-class English accent hardly fitted with the man who'd climbed his way up from the grass roots. But he was unperturbed by his critics: he saw the role as a challenge and was determined to make it a success.

'It's hard to say why I choose to do the films that I do,' he confessed to the *Irish News* in 2016. 'It's hard to say why I play the characters I choose to play. But it's always something instinctive. It's a pure gut feeling.'

He first read the script in 2012 and immediately recognised it was a world away from anything he'd done before: 'There was something in Marc Abraham's script, which I read for the first time four years ago, which seemed incredibly authentic and which I really connected to. Marc had written Hank Williams with such compassion and lack of judgement.'

Completely hooked, he knew he wanted to be part of the project. 'I chose this role because it scared me, and because I love music. It's a huge inspiration. I wasn't sure if I could do this role, and I wanted to see if I could. Maybe that's an expression of my own insanity, this relentless self-challenge.'

Abraham's script had lured him in, and deep down he was aware there was no going back: 'In many respects, I related to Hank's generosity of spirit and Hank's joy at performing, and his very genuine connection with his audience, which I find is true of myself as an actor. It was also about a young man strung in with his own demons. I found the character very compelling, even though I had never sung in my life in a professional capacity. It was just such a meaty challenge. There was so much to get my teeth into that it was irresistible.'

But this was no light undertaking.

'I felt a huge responsibility to Hank Williams and his legacy,' he told reporters.

And he felt this responsibility even more when he arrived in Nashville to prepare for the role. He had forty days to learn how to sing, talk and move like the great musician before filming was due to commence in Shreveport, Louisiana.

The film studio had offered to rent Tom an apartment downtown, but he preferred to stay in the guest room of Rodney Crowell, the music producer for *I Saw the Light*, who would also play Hank's father, Lon.

Tom had started preparations to play Williams long before he'd arrived in Nashville. He was determined to sing all the songs in the film himself. 'I had listened to "Love Sick Blues" and to "Long Gone Lonesome Blues," and I didn't know how to make my vocal cords vibrate to make that specific sound,' he admitted to Rodney's daughter Chelsea Crowell, in an interview for *Rolling Stone* magazine. 'I thought it was an accident of genetics.'

Although he could sing – as demonstrated in his earlier voiceover for *The Pirate Fairy* – he was struggling with this particular gig. Just as he was finishing work on *Crimson Peak* in Toronto, Crowell agreed to fly out and help the actor fine-tune his vocal delivery. The pair sat in Tom's hotel room discussing Williams' life and the effects of his music on people.

'We talked about his extraordinary, instinctive, innate lyricism and natural rhythm and charisma and also his very formidable demons and how those two things possibly come hand in hand,' said Tom. 'And then we talked about the music.'

Crowell taught him about the history of the blues and showed him the 1-4-5 chord progression that is the blueprint of classic country songs. 'Tom, being an educated man, understood the post-war honky-tonk culture that catapulted Hank Williams to superstardom,' said Rodney.

For many years, Hiddleston had been a fan of Hank Williams' music, although he admitted to only really knowing a few of his hits. 'But apart from that I didn't know anything about the details of his life or biography,' he confessed. 'I only knew him as a reference in a Leonard Cohen song: "I said to Hank Williams: how lonely does it get?" in "Tower of Song".'

Now he was developing a deeper understanding of the artist's work.

'Music, without question, is my biggest inspiration,' he told *Rolling Stone*. 'If I could only make people feel what I feel from this music then I'll have done something worthwhile.'

More than rise to his own high expectations, Tom also had a responsibility to deliver a faithful representation of Williams to the stars' fans. It was a nerve-wracking prospect. 'It's like I've turned up in Liverpool and I'm going to play John Lennon,' he told Rodney Crowell. 'In Nashville, people have a very strong opinion about Hank Williams. He's revered as one of the godfathers of American music. So the responsibility to play him honestly, and to satisfy people who care very much about him, was massive.

'He's an inspiration and an icon for so many people, so I don't take that lightly.'

* * *

Tom was well aware he had a lot of work to do, and some days he'd practise singing for up to eight hours without a break.

'Hank's tone is not an easy one to emulate, and I had to refine my yodel and inflect my vowel sounds,' he later confessed to *Nola* website in 2016.

Rodney Crowell was extremely supportive but he gave him some very direct criticism, which the actor fully appreciated. 'Tommy boy, I can hear your English choirboy comin' out now,' he would joke.

To help him really understand the music, Crowell told Tom to try and connect with the lyrics.

At times, though, the frustration was too much for the actor to take. 'I didn't physically punch any walls, but I would have put my own head through one at certain points, I was so frustrated,' he admitted to the *Belfast Telegraph* in 2016. 'I had to change the way I naturally sound to sound like someone else, and also to try and express the sincerity and authenticity of his songs.'

But the hard work paid off, and he was able to record 'Why Don't You Love Me' in an hour. 'I have no idea why I found it so easy,' he said afterwards.

Progress wasn't always so smooth, and it took him nearly two weeks to record 'Lovesick Blues'. He would describe it as his own personal Everest.

'The way he sings it is so strange,' he complained. Being a perfectionist, he had to nail it exactly right.

Crowell worked hard to strip away Tom's English upper-class exterior, to make it sound as if he'd been born in the Deep South.

'Sometimes we referred to Hank as "the Snake,"' Rodney would tell him. 'Like, OK, Tom. You're a good boy, but I need the Snake.'

Although patient and sympathetic, there was no denying Crowell was a tough taskmaster too. 'The rhythm and pitch had to be exact,' recalled Hiddleston. 'And then even when rhythm and pitch had been mastered, I then had to release myself into the attitude of the songs. It wasn't enough just to sing them technically.'

Tom told the website *The Verge*, 'my rendering of the music and the songs had to contain the same emotional commitment that Hank had made. So if they were mournful or sad, the audience had to hear and feel my sadness. And if they were infectious and energetic, then I had to have the same energy, inside what Rodney construed as possible musically.'

Crowell would tell his diligent student: 'Tommy boy, you sang "Lovesick Blues" dead-on, but now you've got to go again, because you've gotta rock it. You've gotta rock.'

Eventually his hard work paid off. 'After a while, the guitar playing, the dialect, the singing, became unconscious,' Tom told *The Verge*. 'Or second nature. I did feel free. I went to the Zen place, I was able to improvise and not worry whether I was going to sound like Hank if I did. You can only do that once you've done the work. It's like most things – you can only drive a car with confidence if you've spent a lot of time behind the wheel of a car. It's the same with horseback riding.

'One morning, I go up to his room and knock. I open the door and it's Hank Williams,' Crowell would later tell journalists. 'These dark slits for eyes. Then, slowly, the Snake receded and it was Tom again. He gave me that chuckle he does and said: "I was in there." He's a very wise young man. A good salt.'

Along with songs, Tom also listened to live recordings and countless radio shows. 'There's so much surviving audio material,' he told *Esquire* magazine. 'I discovered an incredibly charismatic, incredibly witty, and quick, good-humoured and playful person, somebody who had the gift of the gab, who seemed to clearly be huge fun to be around.

'But also I had to try to square that off with the man who said that the sunset was the most lonesome time of the day, which is the expression of someone deeply sad. I find the sunset to be the most relaxing and enjoyable time of the day. To say that, to be so successful and so famous and charismatic, I thought it was interesting that he said that.'

There was a mountain of material to digest, but some-times it was simple lyrics alone that really allowed him to enter the mind of Hank Williams. Although eager to live and breathe the country music star's life, he wasn't prepared to replicate the same self-destruction off-camera though: 'I'm sure there are many actors who would go more method and do it the Williams' way, which is not eat and drink and smoke, but I just don't want to go there. I don't think it would do any good. You completely lose control over what you're doing,' Tom told *Rolling Stone* in 2015.

But he did find a way to explore the singer's darker side and climb into his head, through his alter ego, Luke the Drifter. Williams had used the alias to record religious themed songs and recitations.

'Luke the Drifter was a real revelation for me,' Tom

revealed at the time, 'because it's like suddenly you have a window inside the man. It is something more personal.'

Dissecting William's personality, Hiddleston told *Rolling Stone*: 'He's probably got a hole in his heart that he's trying to fill, which is why he is so desperate to get on the Opry [a country-music stage concert in Nashville] and be a star. He gets to the Opry and realizes there is nothing there, and that's a tragedy in a way. It's like he is so desperate to be in the centre of the limelight, and he gets to the centre of the limelight and he realizes there is no centre. By the time he realizes it, he is too drunk and high and lost – and that's something very real about the human condition. Even though I'm sure he hurt a lot of people indirectly, I don't think he ever meant to. There are some people who just lose control and hurt people in the process. So I kind of love him. I love his irreverence, I love his wit.

'It's like there's a compulsion towards an exploration of darkness or people who have the courage to lean into it and make no apology or request to be liked.'

Tom kept a picture of Williams hanging in his room and several times a day he would stare at it, trying to imagine exactly what it was that made the man tick.

'You're trying to express the common ground between you and the character, which is one of the most extraordinary side effects of having chosen to do this and commit to this as a life,' the actor mused to *Rolling Stone* in 2015. 'You play all these different people and they all share attributes of yourself. So you realize that in some senses as the human race we are all the same, in so many respects. . . You study the specifics of someone, but you're also trying to access the part of you that has those things.'

* * *

Although Tom wasn't prepared to live on a diet of cigarettes and alcohol to emulate Hank Williams, he did engage in a gruelling fitness regime to achieve the singer's gaunt figure. Every day he would wake up and do six hours of singing followed by a ten-mile run.

'He ran 10 miles and cycled 25 miles a day, and all he ate was peanuts and salad,' confirmed co-star Elizabeth Olsen, who was cast as Hank's wife, Audrey, in the film.

Rodney Crowell was equally amazed by the star's commitment and almost superhuman staying power. He told *EOnline*: 'On a typical day in September, I watched him sit for a wardrobe fitting, read through four hours' worth of key scenes with the director and leading lady, spend another two hours with a dialect coach, and then, in order to lose the weight needed to look Hank Williams' gaunt on screen, run seven wicked miles over hilly Tennessee terrain. With those chores done, he'd then commit to six more hours of singing, over and over again, a very hard-to-master song like "Lovesick Blues".

'And then, when he finally unlocked the mystery of yodelling the blues, hillbilly style, and was treated to a playback of his performance responded by saying, "I can do it better, let me go again." Then came a late dinner, wolfed down before giving in to a few hours' sleep.'

* * *

As ever, Tom knew his acting skills alone wouldn't be enough to make the film a success, he also relied on his talented co-stars. He believed Williams' relationship with his wife Audrey fundamentally shaped the singer's music: she had a head for business and really helped kick-start his early career. But after drinking too much alcohol, Williams would often fight with her: 'As Audrey receded into the background, you start to see how Hank kind of goes adrift without that anchor, and I think in quite a fascinating way,' recalled Tom to *Esquire* in 2016. 'Those songs came from the passion of that relationship.

'Hank and Audrey clearly had such a passionate and volatile relationship,' he added. 'They loved each other so much but they were unintentionally cruel to each other.'

Off-camera, he quickly earned his co-star Elizabeth Olsen's respect and she welcomed his tips and advice. She described her time on set as one of the most creative environments she'd ever been in.

'With that kind of safety you're allowed to have intimacy,' she explained to *ETOnline* in 2016. 'You're able to listen to someone and be present within a film together.'

And she had only words of praise for Tom: 'He's a generous spirit,' she told reporters. 'As an actor, he always says, "you don't think about yourself. You think about

who's in front of you. You're trying to get them to respond."
He's a deeply kind person.'

Tom also enjoyed Elizabeth's company – especially on
the tennis court. 'She's such a great tennis partner. She's the
kind of actress who's really in the moment with you. She's
very present. We've been friends for a while so it was nice
to finally work with her,' he told *ETOnline* in 2016.

The two young stars had first met at an audition four years
previously. Even though neither of them got a part in the
film, they both agreed they'd love to work together one day.
The chemistry between them was electric – leading gossip
magazines to suggest a romance was brewing. American
magazine *US Weekly* suggested Tom was 'hooking up'
with the younger sister of the famous Olsen twins: 'The
attractive young star has recently called off her engagement
to actor Boyd Holbrook, but friends emphasized: "She
wants to make a new life for herself. She's having fun."'

Both actors denied they were anything but friends. In
an interview with entertainment news website *ETOnline*,
Olsen dismissed the gossipmongers as 'a bunch of
strangers saying a bunch of stuff that they don't know
about'. Although she did admit working with Tom was
a lot of fun. 'I would love to work with him again,' she
gushed. 'He's such an incredible person. Anyone who's
worked with him knows how disciplined and rigorous he
is, and kind and respectful.'

* * *

Although love didn't spill into real life, there were elements of the film Tom did take beyond the studio – principally, the singing.

Rodney Crowell was due to perform at the Wheatland Music Festival in Michigan. He invited Tom to join him for the ride, and when he overheard him running through the Hank Williams' classic 'I'm So Lonesome I Could Cry', he asked the actor to join him on stage.

A fan uploaded footage of the performance onto YouTube. Although Tom appears calm and collected throughout, he admitted afterwards that the whole thing had been 'absolutely terrifying'.

'I think I may have played the song a little fast,' he complained. 'My inner tempo accelerates.'

But later that night, he got up on stage again to do a rendition of 'Move It On Over'.

'Afterward, brimming with delight, he admitted, rather boyishly, that he'd never in his life performed with a band and had loved it,' said Crowell to BBC America. He was impressed by his student's enthusiasm. 'I was surprised when he said yes and skilfully performed the tune before what must have been 1500 people.'

And he was pleased with the results he was seeing. 'After nearly a month spent collaborating with this gifted artist, I'm as respectful of the man's work ethic as I'm mystified by his transformational skills,' Crowell wrote on his Facebook page beneath a selfie of himself and Hiddleston. 'Without a doubt, the filmmakers chose the right actor for the job.'

Although Tom had never performed as a singer on stage, he could quickly draw parallels with his theatre experience, telling *Esquire* in 2016: 'I think the connection of a performer on stage with a live audience is quite similar. There's an expansion that happens on stage. You realize that you're one man trying to reach hundreds of people. You're out there with the vast expanse of blackness stretching out before you. There's kind of an internal monitor of someone turning up the volume on everything in a way.'

Doing the concert also gave him a greater insight into Williams' character: 'I found that there was a fascinating tension between his exterior charisma and his interior vulnerability. Up on stage, in that spotlight, he's the biggest star in the world, while at home, when he's had a few whiskeys and a fight with his wife, he's deeply lost and alone.'

* * *

While singing was new to Hiddleston, playing the guitar certainly wasn't. He'd been a gifted musician since his school days.

'I took up the guitar when I was at school. I really liked classical guitar initially, but not for very long,' he revealed to *Esquire*. 'When you're at school, you've only got a certain amount of time for extracurricular activities. I played sport and acted in plays and didn't practice guitar, so it became a pastime of leisure. It became the classic sort of noodling around playing "Twist of Fate" by Bob Dylan and any song I thought sounded interesting. I knew the chord progressions and all that, but I never played it professionally or in a band.'

Just before the film was released, Tom even arranged to meet the *Guardian* newspaper in Macari's guitar shop in London to perform a few tracks.

'Anyone who plays the guitar will know it has enormous power,' he said. 'Music is the most immediately infectious art form.'

* * *

Hiddleston's performance in *I Saw the Light* was widely recognised as spellbinding, but unfortunately the film itself fell short of expectations. In fact, it turned out to be one of the worst reviewed in his career to date.

'Of course I put so much into it and it would be lovely to think more people have seen it than I believe they have,' he told *Business Insider*. 'The people I've spoken to about the movie have at least caught the passion for which it was made and then of course there are other people who I don't know personally who have found fault or flaws in it, but I can't be the judge. Everyone is entitled to their own opinion. As an actor, you just have to put your best foot forward every time.

'But the experience of making that film was so pleasurable that I'll always have it. It was a huge labour of love. I spent over five months of my life making it, thinking about it every minute of every day. That's what it's like making films. You commit a huge amount of time and energy to make things and it only takes two hours for anyone in the audience, whether they like it or not.'

'The only thing that matters to me is the work,' he would later reveal. 'Other people's opinions of me are things I can't control, and that's all fame really is, a collection of other people's opinions.

'I can only control who I am, and how I commit to the work, and how I am in the world. And how that's reflected or refracted through other people is their business.'

Besides, no matter how the film was received, it had occupied a very important six months of his life. It was refreshing to tackle an arthouse movie after doing a flurry of blockbusters.

'Big-budget films... you have more time. And for smaller budgets, you shoot more quickly. That can be a good thing and a bad thing. There can be things you feel you missed because you were going so fast, but sometimes too much time gives you too much time to think and question and look from every angle and then you can't commit to the best choice,' he told *Business Insider* in 2016.

No matter how big a production he was making, Tom enjoyed every acting job that came his way. With every character he played, he always found he'd end up learning something new about himself. He told *The Verge* in 2016, 'I suppose it's expressing different sides of myself. But also, I hope the stories, the characterisations, illuminate aspects of the human condition which are universal. We're all capable of courage and heroism. We've all experienced joy, we've all felt pain.

'And every time I go to work, that's really what I'm trying to communicate. Whether I'm playing Loki, or Hank Williams, or F. Scott Fitzgerald, or Coriolanus, or Henry V, or Jonathan Pine [*The Night Manager*], I hope there's some expression of something that people relate to.'

By the time the film was released, it felt like the actor Tom Hiddleston was everywhere. Due to release schedules, *Crimson Peak*, *High-Rise* and *I Saw the Light* were released in quick succession.

Tom said in an interview at the time: 'I apologize, unreservedly, first of all, for being everywhere. I'm sure it's deeply tiresome and nobody wants to ever see my face again. There's a strange coincidence in that the work of the last 18 months of my life has all been released at the same time. And for me, each piece of work has such integrity and focus. But it must seem different to be in the audience. I do feel very lucky that I'm allowed to do so many different things.'

CHAPTER FIFTEEN

THE NIGHT MANAGER

While seemingly dominating the big screen, Tom was also having a decent stab at commanding the world of TV. British audiences were the first to see six-part series *The Night Manager* when it aired on BBC1 on 21 February 2016. It would be screened several months later in America and then sold to more than 180 countries.

The drama was an adaptation of John le Carré's 1993 espionage novel, which revolves around former British soldier Jonathan Pine, who has fought in Iraq and is now retreating from life by working in a luxury hotel. He is recruited by intelligence operative Angela Burr (Olivia Colman) to infiltrate Whitehall and Washington and bring down an arms dealer (played by Hugh Laurie).

Director Susanne Bier had modified the story to make it resonate with a contemporary audience, switching it from the Cold War period to a modern-day era dominated by South American drug lords and the bloody aftermath of the Arab Spring. It would be the first adaptation of a le Carré novel in more than twenty years.

'In order for the show to have the same impact as the book, it had to speak to our political climate now; updated and wedded to the world we live in,' Hiddleston said.

Meanwhile Susanne Bier described the character of Jonathan Pine as 'a deeply romantic character but a closed human being. In the course of becoming a real spy he then becomes an actual human being as well'.

Hugh Laurie, who was cast as arms dealer Richard Onslow Roper, described by John le Carré in his novel as 'the worst man in the world', had actually tried to secure the rights to make the book into a film when it was initially published but he discovered they were already owned by the director Sydney Pollack. When he passed away in 2008, the rights reverted to le Carré's sons. When Laurie discovered they were planning to make a TV adaptation of the story, he quickly jumped on board as a lead and executive producer.

'I tried to option the book. I was far too late, and the great Sydney Pollack had it,' he revealed to *Time* magazine. 'The world turns, and 20-odd years later it comes back to life, by which point of course I'm far too old and creaky and bald to play Jonathan Pine, but we have to resign ourselves to these processes.'

* * *

Tom first received he script while in the midst of movie making. His agent had told him that Simon and Stephen Cornwell, John le Carré's sons, were currently seeking actors for a TV adaptation of *The Night Manager* novel.

'I read the first episode, and from the very beginning, I was completely hooked into the story and the character. I fell in love with it immediately,' Hiddleston told the BBC in 2016.

'It was a breath-taking and mouth-watering prospect,' he added. 'I never like to go over the same territory twice and I'm always looking for new things and new characters.'

The character of Jonathan Pine appealed to him because he knew he'd have to 'operate at the highest level of my intellectual and physical ability' to fulfil the role: 'I found his nobility, courage and morality very appealing – he is actually a very moral character and is filled with le Carré's own moral authority about the world. There is a certain line that you can feel underneath all of le Carré's work which is a very robust moral foundation: a belief in right and wrong; in decency and its opposite.'

Tom was also inspired by Jonathan Pine's bravery in the field. He thought of all the other similar real-life heroes out there who have fought in wars or put their lives on the line to gather intelligence. Although he had never read the novel before, he went straight out and found a copy of the book, devouring every page.

'I think John le Carré occupies a unique position in British literature and storytelling. I think he has a singular authority on the subject matter, having been in the circus himself, as they say. He is a deeply gifted narrative storyteller and a master of his art, the espionage thriller. I think the reason any actor would be drawn to an adaptation of his material is the characters, which are incredibly complex, incredibly rich and as surprising and contradictory as real people are.'

He recalled reading a description of the character from le Carré's novel: 'There's a fantastic paragraph at the opening of chapter three of the novel, where Jonathan Pine is described as [a] "graduate of a rainy archipelago of orphanages and foster homes, a sometime army wolf child, a collector of other people's languages, a perpetual escapee from emotional entanglement, a self-exiled creature of the night and a sailor without destination". I clung to those words, because I think there's so many clues in there.'

He even read the section of the book to his sisters, Emma and Sarah, and they immediately shouted back: 'That's you!'

Describing the book to journalists, Tom said: 'At the beginning of the story, he [Pine] is a lost soul. He is the night manager of a 5-Star hotel in the ski resort of Zermatt in the Swiss Alps, living an almost monastic life, literally and figuratively buried in snow, silence and darkness. I think he is a mystery to all men and to himself – the uniform and the face he prepares to meet others is a mask that protects him from having to know who he is.

'Behind an immaculate three-piece suit, immaculate tie, polished black shoes and impeccable manners, he almost has no character because he is filled with guilt and shame because of what has happened in his past. He is a former soldier who has served two tours in Iraq, so though he has disbanded from the military, he is still a serviceman – he is just serving in the hotel now as opposed to in the army.'

In the TV adaptation Jonathan Pine was the hotel manager of a luxury property in Cairo, just at the time of the Arab Spring, when riots were breaking out.

'Jonathan Pine is trying to get people out of the hotel,' explained Tom. 'In the midst of the chaos, an event occurs. He is introduced to an MI6 agent and recruited to join them as a spy.'

As background research, he shadowed the night manager of the five-star Rosewood Hotel in London, following him and watching his every move. 'I found the performance fascinating,' he said. 'The manager had impeccable courtesy. If somebody asks where the bar is, you say: "Allow me to escort you." It's about making every guest feel looked after.'

The series was shot in a number of different locations. Filming began in March 2015 in Zermatt, Switzerland, and moved to London, Devon, Marrakesh, Morocco and Majorca.

'The locations have been amazing, truly,' Tom told reporters at the BBC. 'This story has enormous scale and ambition and the locations we have been to have added so much texture to that.

'Often I turned up on set and had a very reassuring feeling as my imagination didn't have to supply anything else because I had been placed immediately in a completely believable context for where the character is. Each location has been so immaculately designed and so correctly chosen it often took our breath away.'

* * *

Tom thrived on the excitement and fast pace of moving between so many locations at such a relentless pace.

'I just loved the experience of making it,' he told his friend and fellow actor Benedict Cumberbatch, when the *Sherlock* star was invited to interview Tom for *Interview* magazine in September 2016. 'It always felt as though we were making a six-hour feature. We storyboarded it and scheduled it as one 360-page screenplay, with one director. Susanne [Bier] was our captain. We shot in Switzerland, London, Devon, Morocco, and Majorca, in that order.

'It felt like the lion's share of the series took place in Morocco, in Marrakesh, where our Cairo interiors were, and where we shot the Arab Spring riots. We spent seven weeks in Marrakesh and we had to get through so many pages per day, in which I was featured in every frame, jumping between identities – I was Jonathan Pine and Andrew Birch and Thomas Quince and Jack Linden.

'Someone asked me recently what was it like to go back to television, and it didn't feel like that. The difference is greater for the audience than it is for us, I think.'

On set, the actor was a ball of energy. 'Tom never stops running. Before work, after work, during work,' revealed his co-star, Hugh Laurie. 'And it adds hugely to the common tank of energy that a film crew runs on. Every time someone yawns, or scratches their arse, the crew leaks a little energy – Tom's the one who tops it up.'

Describing the relationship between Richard Onslow Roper and Jonathan Pine, Hiddleston joked, 'It's a burgeoning bromance. They're drawn to each other. But at the same time there's a very sophisticated game of cat and mouse, and you're constantly guessing who is the cat and who is the mouse.

'It's much more complex than the division of good and evil because Pine and Roper like each other, but Roper is a cynic and a nihilist, while Pine has a moral sensor. And that tension is played out under this umbrella of British manners and hypocrisy.'

Hugh Laurie described Pine as 'an errant knight in search of a cause'.

Tom spent a long time mulling over what it meant to be a spy. The idea fascinated him: 'The challenge of what makes a good spy is their ability to dissemble, and they are able to capitalize on the flexibility and malleability of their identity in a way that is self-eradicating. I think there is a fascinating question there about identity.

'If a man is so flexible and so credible in concealment and revelation, who is he really? The solitude is profound, and the obligation is to live without the privilege of intimate relationships. There is no one with whom you can share your inner life. For many of us, that's what we live for – having people in our lives we can open up to.'

He even wrote an article on the topic, published in the *Radio Times* when the programme was airing in February 2016.

Social media capture the first spark of public opinion – something funny, more often something outrageous, occasionally something kind – whip it into a viral trend, and the flame grows with increasing intensity until it spreads around the world like wildfire.

This takes place in a matter of seconds. Like a murmuration of starlings, the swell of public voices can change shape seemingly of its own accord, with a newly reinforced power – at times to celebrate and unify, at others to humiliate and divide. It's a miracle that there are any secrets left. Everything is everyone's business. Which begs the question: in today's world, how could one possibly get away with being a spy?

He went on to discuss intelligence in modern-day politics:

To my mind, it feels as though there are still so many secrets, so many private conversations behind closed doors in the corridors of power. I don't doubt that the business of government and the intelligence and security services remains undisclosed in the interests of national security and international relations. But their work remains opaque and mysterious.

There is, behind the curtain, a complex network of

interests and relationships, upon which depend our national security. This milieu is le Carré's métier.

The eloquently written piece was well received and earned the educated actor even greater respect. But it seemed many fans were interested in something other than Hiddleston's brain... *The Night Manager* featured several scenes of nudity, which sent social media into a spiral.

In one scene, Tom was filmed running along Devon's cliff-tops, and stripping off for a shower beneath a waterfall. A sex scene between Jonathan Pine and Jed Marshall (played by Elizabeth Debicki) also elicited a frenzied response in the tabloids.

Jonathan pushes Jed against the wall and pulls down his trousers, giving viewers an eyeful of Tom's 'peachy behind'.

'Oh my god the fates have smiled on me with that sex scene...what a peachy backside,' wrote one user on Twitter.

While another added: 'Is anyone else steaming from that super sexy sex scene just now on #TheNightManager? Blimey...'

Another Tweet read: 'I want sex against a wall with tom hiddleston.'

While another said: 'Never mind John Le Carre's cameo in tonight's #TheNightManagers what about @twhiddleston's bottom?'

The excitement sent the hashtag Hiddlesbum trending on Twitter.

The actor was quick to play down any fuss when asked

about the scene in interviews. 'There's a love scene. In the room at the time, with Elizabeth Debicki and myself, are 15 strong men lifting heavy machinery – so it doesn't feel real,' he explained.

But censors in the US obviously disagreed. When the miniseries was shown on the AMC Channel, glimpses of Hiddleston's backside were removed.

'I was surprised to hear that they cut my butt out!' the actor told *W* magazine. 'I'm here to tell you that my butt is not dangerous. And there are many, many more dangerous things that people are happy to broadcast. I don't know what that says about the world we live in, but it probably says something.'

Meanwhile Tom's loyal fans, the Hiddlestoners, still found a way to access the scenes. The actor was still baffled by his growing fan base, though deeply flattered. In particular, it was the term 'Hiddlestoner' which he found odd.

'I always found it slightly disconcerting,' he told ABC News, 'because it reminded me of that scene in *Life of Brian*, where they go to a stoning and people are physically stoned!' But he realised that many of his young fans had actually broadened their minds through being so dedicated.

'Many are really into the work; they follow me into some interesting corners. When it was announced I was doing *High-Rise*, they read the book; when I was appearing in *Coriolanus*, they came to see the play. So it's nice to know you're introducing people to new things.'

The Night Manager was a huge success in the UK, with comments flooding the internet after every episode. Tom took it as a great compliment when fans would stop him in the street and gush about how much they loved the programme.

'People seem to want to watch it in one or two sittings,' he said. 'It feels like a story that has its own propulsive momentum, and that's honestly how it was designed.

'It took me a year [to shoot] and all it takes is six hours [to watch],' he joked, emphasising how much more time he'd invested in the series. 'But that's OK. That's making art.

'It takes people a long time to make things. It takes people a long time to cut records and paint paintings. That's just the nature of making stuff.'

In America, the critics couldn't help but draw comparisons with James Bond.

'Beyond the globetrotting tale, the opening credits mimic the imagery that made the Bond films so iconic,' wrote *Time* magazine. 'Hiddleston even orders a vodka Martini while sporting a smart suit at the end of the final episode.'

Given the speculation Daniel Craig might be stepping down from the lead role, Tom Hiddleston seemed to be an obvious choice, given his British heritage and expertise at playing a spy.

Shortly after his fourth Bond movie, *Spectre*, was released in 2015, Daniel Craig told the press he would 'rather slash my wrists' than reprise the role again.

'I'm over it at the moment,' he told *Time Out* magazine. 'We're done. All I want to do is move on.'

Although he quickly gave himself a get-out clause and said this would be his view 'for at least a year or two'.

But rumours of a new Bond resurfaced. According to the *Daily Mail* newspaper, a source had revealed: 'Daniel is done – pure and simple – he told top brass at MGM after *Spectre*. They threw huge amounts of money at him, but it just wasn't what he wanted.

'He had told people after shooting that this would be his final outing,' the source continued, 'but the film company still felt he could come around after *Spectre* if he was offered a money deal.'

Apparently having turned his back on a two-film deal worth £68 million, Daniel Craig had allegedly left the door to Bond open wide.

Initially, though, Tom denied he'd been approached. Appearing on *The Graham Norton Show*, he said: 'The position isn't vacant as far as I'm aware. No one has talked to me about it.

'I think the rumours have come about because in *The Night Manager* I play a spy and people have made the link.'

'It is similar,' he admitted, when asked by *Esquire* to draw comparisons between *The Night Manager* and Bond. 'He's a British spy, with a military history; he's a solitary figure, heroic, he's in a tight spot...

'But they are rather different. Bond is a trained killer with a 00 license. Pine is someone who's beginning his experience as a field agent. And I think John le Carré's characters more than those of [Bond writer] Ian Fleming are haunted by moral ambivalence.

'I'd make a terrible spy, because everybody knows who I am. But [director] Susanne Bier said that she thinks I am very enigmatic and good at keeping secrets.'

Continuing the obvious connections, one critic even suggested Hugh Laurie should play 007: 'I am not familiar with the mental health of this person, but that's the craziest thing I've ever heard,' laughed Hugh. 'I can't climb stairs without my knees popping. I'm not the guy to be hurling myself out of helicopters, if indeed I ever was.'

When quizzed by *Esquire* magazine, Tom refused to spill any beans on the matter, but he did confess to being a fan of the Bond franchise. His favourite movie was *From Russia With Love*, and he said he understood why 007 was such a national obsession: 'I think it's because he represents an archetype. There's this idea of British strength which doesn't draw attention to itself but gets the job done,' he told *Esquire*.

'That's our brand. We know it's inelegant to blow your own trumpet and impolite to show how much you care, and yet we expect you to win! You don't find it in France or Spain. Captain America is dressed in the American flag – the heroism is so much more overt. But Bond is debonair, detached, good humoured, well mannered, efficient, charming...'

While Hiddleston remained tight-lipped about any new job prospects, his fans eagerly highlighted his ability to tackle the role. Even his *High-Rise* co-star Sienna Miller thought he was a sure bet for the job.

'Oh wow, he should be, he totally could do that! He is Bond, isn't he?' she told the *Belfast Telegraph* in 2016.

In a November 2015 poll by *Time* magazine readers on who should land the role after Daniel Craig, Tom was in twelfth position.

'*Time* magazine ran a poll and there were, like, 100 actors on the list, including Angelina Jolie. But, yes, it's nice to be included in the 100,' the actor admitted.

'I'm a huge fan of the series. I'm very aware of the physicality of the job. I would not take it lightly.

'I simply love the theme tune, the tropes and the mythology,' he added. 'I love the whole thing. If it ever came knocking, it would be an extraordinary opportunity.'

Some critics, however, didn't feel he had the prowess to take on the role. 'The torso is not enough, Mr Wannabe Bond,' wrote Camilla Long in the *Sunday Times*. 'It's incredibly difficult to cast a new Bond because it is almost impossible to find a British actor who doesn't look completely stupid holding a gun.

'It is why dull Hiddleston and duller Damian Lewis fall short. All of them have gym tits; but none of them has the cold-blooded panther prowl of a searing god with a glinting Walther PPK.'

Meanwhile the bookmakers Coral were taking bets on whether Tom Hiddleston would be the next Bond, although they closed the book when it was reported the actor had met with Bond director Sam Mendes and producer Barbara Broccoli at the Soho House private members' club in London. There was no evidence, though, to substantiate the claims.

By now, though, Tom was getting fed up with the rumours. 'It's all speculation!' he complained to *Hello!* magazine. 'Wondering who's going to play the next Bond has become a national pastime!'

'I feel like, I want to just make it stop,' he told *Sky News*. 'Because I have no power over it, but that's what being famous is. You have no power over other people's opinions.

'People have very strong opinions about Bond and why shouldn't they? But it's difficult to talk about because it's a completely unreal conversation in a way.

'It's odd because it's becoming overwhelming – not the thing of it, but the number of people per day who bring it up. It's actually becoming a weird thing to deal with.

'It's just an idea in people's minds so it's quite hard to engage with because it hasn't come from me if that makes sense.'

For now, the idea of Bond seemed a long way off – or at least that was the impression Tom was giving people. 'I don't think that announcement is coming, but I am very gratified to hear the enthusiasm. Your guess is as good as mine, to be honest,' he told reporters.

CHAPTER SIXTEEN

'HIDDLESWIFT'

It would be all too easy to believe that compared to making a feature film, recording a TV miniseries would be far less stressful. Given the high production value of *The Night Manager* (each episode cost an estimate £3 million to make according to a report in the *Telegraph*), that wasn't the case at all.

One of John le Carré's sons, Simon Cornwell, whose company, Ink Factory, had collaborated on the project with BBC and US TV channel AMC, admitted it had been a 'risk'. But it was a gamble that had paid off. 'It's a difficult book to adapt,' he told *BBC News*, 'and there have been quite a few attempts to make it into a film, it just didn't work. It needed six hours to explain the story.

'But to all intents and purposes it's been written and shot as a film – we just hired one director, Susanne Bier, for all six episodes. I always think of it as a film – just a six-hour one.'

He acknowledged Tom's starring role in *The Night Manager* had been instrumental to the series' success.

'We hired a superstar in the making. I don't think British audiences have ever had so much screen time with Tom Hiddleston before.

'Viewers have been able to tune in week after week to see him and have become invested in his character, and with him.

'What's great for me is when I go and get lunch in cafes and I overhear people talking about him in the latest episode – that's when it hits you how popular the show is.'

Hiddleston himself had enjoyed every minute of the filming, but once the cameras stopped rolling, he was left feeling exhausted. 'When I finished *The Night Manager*, I realized that, for 75 days, I had lived more hours per day as Jonathan Pine than I had spent as myself,' he told his friend Benedict Cumberbatch in an interview for *Interview* magazine in 2016. 'You're putting yourself into this other person's shoes. The best thing I could have done was exactly what I did. I flew home and I went to my sister's engagement party. I was surrounded by family. And they were so reassuring.'

He relished the opportunity to potter around at home, read books and catch up with his friends and family over coffees.

'I live such a boring life!' he laughed.

Home was now a four-bedroom house in London's Primrose Hill, which was once an artist's studio. According to reports in the *Daily Mail* newspaper, it was 'every inch the movie-star's place – a knockout'. Guests had to enter through electronic gates and two separate courtyards to reach the £5 million property.

When asked about the place, Tom revealed it was full of books – although he also stressed he had limited possessions: 'When I was 27, I travelled a lot for work. I'd return to my London flat and feel uncomfortable in it because I had too much stuff.

'On the advice of my friend [actress] Rebecca Hall, I got rid of all my belongings and lived out of two suitcases for 12 months. It was the most enjoyable year of my life.'

Although he surrounded himself with friends and family whenever he could, being on the road for long periods at a time meant it was tough for him to develop relationships. Some unnamed acquaintances hinted that he was something of a chameleon when it came to women; he'd only allow them to get so close and then he'd move on. But growing up in a household of females had taught him a great deal about the opposite sex. He credited his two sisters, Emma and Sarah, for teaching him how to treat women properly.

'The first lesson was always to compliment them on their new haircut,' he told *Hello!* magazine. 'And always to support them in whatever they're doing. My sisters are very strong-minded, independent women – as is my mother – and I've learnt a lot about women from them.

'When I was 16, I noticed I had friends who had grown up exclusively around men, and they didn't understand women at all. I like to think that through growing up with my sisters, I have a sense of who women are, of their needs, their diversity and all those lovely things.'

Over the past few years he had been romantically linked with a few women, but no concrete evidence of any lasting relationships had really emerged.

All that, though, was about to change...

* * *

Already a big name on both sides of the Atlantic, Tom was constantly bombarded with invitations to prestigious awards ceremonies or lavish parties. Quite often, he'd be too busy to attend, or he'd politely decline in favour of spending more quality time with those closest to him. However, one invitation caught his attention. He'd been asked to attend the Met Gala Ball (a fashion equivalent of the Oscars) at the Metropolitan Museum of Art in New York on 2 May 2016. The invitation also extended to a pre-ball dinner at *Vogue* editor-in-chief Anna Wintour's home the night before.

The A-list fashion guru had always been a fan of Hiddleston's work. Only a month earlier at a launch for *The Night Manager* in the US, Wintour had raised a glass and said: 'Some actors are chameleons... Others are so charismatic that they just get to play variations on a persona, while some are just ridiculously good-looking! Tom is all three.'

The humble star replied: 'You leave me bashful and tongue-tied.'

On the night of the pre-Met Ball dinner, he joined an array of stars gathered at Wintour's home, including fellow actor Idris Elba and the singer-songwriter Taylor Swift. At the time Swift was dating DJ and producer Calvin Smith, but observers quickly clocked how well she was getting on with Tom. Photographs later emerged of Taylor looking longingly at him from the doorstep of Wintour's house just as he was leaving with Idris Elba at the end of the evening.

The following night, the pair connected again at the ball. Taylor was dressed in a metallic snakeskin-effect Louis Vuitton minidress, topped off with dark plum lipstick and strappy heels wrapping around to her knees; Tom had opted for a classic dinner suit and looked every bit the English gentleman.

As the evening wore on, and awards had been presented, guests started to let their hair down. Taylor and Tom made a beeline for each other, and as soon as the opportunity arose, they hit the dance floor. Footage of the pair showing off their moves was secretly filmed and uploaded to Instagram, where it went instantly viral.

When Tom was later asked about the episode, all he could do was smile. 'I love dancing – who doesn't?' he told reporters. 'It's a weird one. I haven't actually danced for a long time, but I happened to be dancing at the Met Gala because it was a party.

'I was on a table with Taylor Swift and The Weeknd was

playing, and she said, "The thing about these parties is nobody gets up to dance." And she, as a musician, was like, "We've got to dance for The Weeknd", so we got up and danced.

'She said: "If they play 'I Can't Feel My Face' we have to get up and dance as an encore."

'I said: "I'm in, of course, let's go. Absolutely." We just jumped up and started dancing – and everybody else started dancing – which was great. And it was cool. Taylor is a huge star. Maybe it's just the randomness of it.

'I didn't know it was going to ping round the world, but it's all good.'

The pair had obviously hit it off. Tom told MTV: 'I sat next to her at dinner that night and she's very charming, she's amazing. I've seen a couple of her videos. I think "Shake It Off" was released around the time we made *I Saw the Light*, and she's very cool.'

But he quickly added: 'I don't know that I could stand up to her vocal talents.'

* * *

Shortly after the party, Taylor cancelled an appearance at the Billboard Music Awards and dashed to the bedside of her Scottish boyfriend Calvin Harris (real name Adam Wiles) after he was injured in a car accident in Las Vegas in May 2016 just before he was due to DJ. He was being driven to the airport when a 16-year-old girl crashed her Volkswagen Beetle into his 4x4, leaving him with facial cuts.

Only a month earlier, the pair had celebrated their one-year anniversary with a romantic holiday in the Caribbean and in an interview with *Vogue*, Taylor had gushed about their 'magical relationship'. The pair had posted loved-up images on Instagram, showing them in a series of sun-splashed embraces; they were pictured kissing at sunset, taking a piggyback and floating around a pool in an inflatable swan.

'That time when we finally took a vacation. @calvinharris,' Taylor wrote.

When asked whether marriage was on the cards she revealed: 'I'm just taking things as they come. I'm in a magical relationship right now. And of course I want it to be ours, and low-key . . . this is the one thing that's been mine about my personal life.'

But that idyllic picture was soon to be shattered. On 1 June 2016 they announced the relationship was over. Calvin tweeted: 'The only truth here is that a relationship came to an end & what remains is a huge amount of love and respect.' Within two hours his statement was retweeted 18,000 times by users – including Taylor Swift.

An insider suggested Calvin had called time on the relationship, saying: 'He wasn't ready to settle down for good but they are hoping to remain friends. Neither of them wants an acrimonious break-up – or a bitter break-up album.'

Apparently the relationship was getting too intense.

'Things just got a bit too heavy for him. Taylor is very intense professionally, and on a personal level too.

'She's a great girl but she's used to having things her way – and Adam is not a yes-man.'

The Sun newspaper, however, claimed it was Taylor who had instigated the break-up after the DJ refused to commit to marriage and kids.

According to a report in *Reveal* magazine, Tom called Taylor immediately the announcement was made to console her, and they spoke for almost an hour. While on the phone he also managed to order flowers, which arrived shortly after they hung up. But several weeks later there was a new twist in the drama when pictures emerged of Taylor Swift kissing Tom Hiddleston at her home on Rhode Island, New England.

The Sun newspaper splashed a series of photographs across its front page with the headline: 'Tinker Taylor Snogs a Spy'. The stars were pictured kissing, while sat on rocks overlooking the Atlantic Ocean.

The Misquamicut State Beach, close to Taylor's £12 million, eight-bedroom mansion in Watch Hill, was one of her favourite spots. At one point, chivalrous Tom gave Taylor his jacket to keep her warm, and they posed for several selfies on their mobile phones.

'They were all over each other – hugging and kissing – even though there were 20 people coming and going on the beach,' revealed an unnamed source to *The Sun* newspaper. 'They looked like any young couple madly in love without a care in the world.'

A source told the *Daily Star*: 'There was an immediate

attraction. She felt like she was a little schoolgirl with a huge crush. She loves the fact that Tom acts like such a mature man. She loves that he is older. She feels very safe and protected with him.'

* * *

Initially, Tom refused to talk about the fledgling love affair. Meanwhile one computer whizz stitched together excerpts from old interviews to make it look like the actor was talking about his relationship with Taylor, describing it as 'a rollercoaster ride of action and spectacle and lots of laughs'.

It later emerged the interview was a fake.

A spokesman for Hiddleston said: 'It's a fake interview, stitched together from old interview snippets to make it appear new.'

Although Swift's agents claimed no one else had been involved in her break-up with Calvin Harris, these new images seemed to suggest otherwise. Even if nothing between Tom and Taylor had actually happened until after the split, the timing wasn't great.

Calvin was apparently 'aware' of the pictures and when asked in an interview with *Vanity Fair* in September 2016 about his ex he said: 'She's doing her own thing.' Shortly afterwards, he unfollowed the singer and her younger brother Austin on social media, and tweeted the gnomic statement, 'Oh boy it's about to go down' along with three skull emojis. Soon afterwards he deleted the Tweet, though.

Taylor responded by deleting all her pictures taken during the relationship.

Meanwhile, her new relationship with Tom was storming ahead at full speed. The couple were next photographed together in Nashville, where they headed to see Taylor's friend American actress-singer Selena Gomez play live, along with Taylor's brother, Austin, and his best friend, Abigail Anderson. Instagram footage showed them hugging and dancing in the stadium.

While visiting her hometown, Taylor also seized the opportunity to introduce Tom to her parents, Scott and Andrea. They spent several hours together and then joined friends, Holly Williams and her husband, for dinner at Adele's restaurant (Holly was the daughter of Hank Williams Jr.).

'They looked like they were having an amazing time,' a source told *US* magazine. 'Taylor was laughing at Tom's jokes.'

The pair were also spotted kissing and holding hands during the meal, which included meatballs and kale salad.

On social media, meanwhile, Calvin Harris decided it was time he said a few words. He claimed he was not jealous of the relationship, but just 'free'.

Meanwhile the Hiddleswift juggernaut showed no signs of slowing down. Days after they'd been in Nashville, the couple flew to England to meet Tom's parents, Diana and James. Pictures emerged in the tabloids, showing Tom and

Taylor walking hand in hand along the pebbled shoreline of Aldeburgh Beach in Suffolk while deep in conversation with Tom's mum, Diana.

Tom also hired a Jaguar F-Type to show her around the English countryside, before they lunched with Diana in Ipswich. Several burly bodyguards escorted the pair around the sleepy coastal town.

'There's lots of tourists about but we don't get people as famous as her,' David, an Aldeburgh resident, told *Now* magazine. 'The young people knew her but most of us were clueless. We know Tom and that's it.'

'There were at least eight photographers running around after them both,' revealed another source. 'We spotted Taylor and Tom with the police before they drove off with Taylor's bodyguards following behind in a Range Rover. It was really hectic but Taylor looked like she was really friendly and stopped to chat with people she saw.'

Diana decided to impress her son's new girlfriend with a home-cooked lunch.

'I cut a fillet steak for Taylor,' local butcher Alfie told *Now* magazine. 'Tom's mum came into our shop and ordered three fillet steaks and said they were for Tom and Taylor. I said "Taylor Swift?" and she said yes. I made sure I gave Taylor a meaty portion when I found out it was for her.'

The visit was reportedly a success.

'Despite being one of the most famous women on the planet, Taylor is very much a homebody,' an unnamed source told *The Sun*. 'Meeting Tom's folks on the Suffolk coast, and going for long walks along the beach, was a perfect picture for her. It was cosy and intimate, like a movie love story.'

But Tom and Taylor's grand tour didn't end there. They got back on Taylor's private jet and headed for Rome, Italy, where they toured some of the eternal city's top sights, and were pictured visiting the Colosseum. They were even photographed kissing inside the UNESCO World Heritage site.

During lunch in a cafe later that day, Tom was seen kissing his girlfriend's hand. They were also spotted walking through the Vatican.

A source told *E!* the blonde beauty had 'texted her close friends and said, "I think I am in love and I never felt this way before!"' The insider added: 'She is having a blast traveling with him. He is very romantic and attentive towards her. He is extremely charming.

'He also makes sure she feels safe wherever they go together. She is on cloud nine and really enjoying this quality time they are spending.'

But users on social media weren't quite so complimentary. Several conspiracy theories suggested the relationship might be a sham, used to distract attention away from a bitter feud Taylor was currently having with Kim Kardashian and Kanye West, or perhaps to further enhance Tom Hiddleston's career. There was also a rumour Taylor might have a new album due for release.

Journalists pointed out that all the photos from their

romantic 'world' tour had come from the same photo agency, indicating they may have been tipped off.

The relationship certainly caused a media frenzy. Social media was awash with suggested names for the couple: Tom-Lor, Swiddleston, The Swiddler, Hiddleswift…

'Hiddleswift. It sounds like some arcane practice out of JK Rowling,' wrote Andrew Anthony in the *Observer*, 'but it is, of course, the latest celebrity hybrid that takes its place alongside those other magnificent centaurs, Brangelina, Bennifer and Kimye.'

Ed Potton, writing for *The Times* newspaper, declared, 'Swift and Hiddleston could be about to rival Brangelina as the world's highest-profile couple. It's fantasy stuff: America's favourite big sister – winner of 10 Grammys, 40 million albums sold – falls for Britain's most eligible bachelor actor, star of *The Night Manager* and possible Bond-in-waiting. Fans, her Swifties and his Hiddlestoners, are going into meltdown. It has the air of a romance created by algorithm, calculated to create the perfect media storm.'

That storm further intensified when Tom attended Taylor's 4 July party at her mansion on Rhode Island. Other guests included Blake Lively, Ryan Reynolds, Gigi Hadid, Karlie Kloss, Cara Delevingne and Ruby Rose. Pictures of the celeb-filled bash were plastered all over social media.

Model and actress Cara Delevingne posted a picture of Tom and Taylor zooming down a waterslide, Taylor clasping her arms tightly around her new boyfriend's toned abs and screaming with laughter. They were also caught kissing in a Polaroid shot, and joined in a very cosy couples photo with Britany LaManna and her husband Benjamin plus Blake Lively and Ryan Reynolds. Perched on a wicker chair on a veranda, Taylor sits on Tom's lap and looks into his eyes as he returns the gaze while dangling a wine glass.

But best of all was a shot featuring Tom in the sea with Taylor. The British actor had even gone so far as to wear an 'I heart TS' vest, announcing his love for the singer once and for all. (Although some Twitter users claimed the initials actually stood for T.S. Eliot, one of Hiddleston's favourite poets.)

Other fans described the display as 'cringeworthy', with still more adding that Tom had 'lost all appeal and credibility'.

One wrote: 'I can only assume Tom Hiddleston lost some form of bet', while another, Elise, declared he 'shouldn't be allowed to be Bond after wearing that s**t t-shirt.'

Tom was also seen sporting a temporary tattoo on his arm with the letter 'T' at the centre.

The 4 July party was a riotous affair. Cara Delevingne later revealed she'd scared Tom and Taylor senseless one night after playing a prank: 'They got woken up, and they came upstairs and Uzo was over in the corner with a light in her hand, holding a speaker. I was throwing myself on the floor punching things, and they were like "AHHH!" Like screaming, and they were like, "Let's go back downstairs, and leave this scene." [Tom] was peeing himself in the corner.'

* * *

The next stop for the golden couple in their whirlwind romance was Australia, where Tom was filming the new *Thor* movie.

Journalists were by now obsessed by his relationship with Taylor Swift and were desperate to dig up some gossip. They even stopped him while he was out jogging on the street to quiz him about the relationship.

'How's Taylor enjoying the beautiful Gold Coast?' asked one reporter.

'Erm, I'm not going to answer that, if that's alright,' he replied.

Meanwhile Taylor tried to remain undercover, but was photographed shopping and also on a movie date to see the new *Ghostbusters* film with the *Thor* cast.

Eventually, it was time to break the silence and Tom gave his first official interview on Taylor to *The Hollywood Reporter*. Responding to rumours the romance was nothing more than a publicity stunt, he said: 'Well, um. How best to put this? The truth is that Taylor Swift and I are together, and we're very happy. Thanks for asking. That's the truth. It's not a publicity stunt.'

Even their immediate circle started discussing the relationship in public. Talking about the effect of Taylor on his friend, Chris Hemsworth revealed: 'I've seen Tom around, he looks happy, mate, yeah!'

But rumours the relationship was nothing more than a cynical ploy to divert attention from the very public spat between Kanye West and Taylor Swift continued to abound.

'It comes down to being authentic,' Tom told *People* magazine. 'Everything you do, you have to make sure you truly believe in it and as long as you know that, it doesn't matter what anyone else says about it because the nature of being a public figure is that everyone will have an opinion about anything you do, and as long as you know why you've done something and you've committed to it with authenticity then you're okay.'

He also finally joined Instagram, uploading a picture of himself as Loki as a teaser to fans for the next instalment in the *Thor* series, *Thor: Ragnarok*, due for release in 2017.

Robert Downey Jr. teased the actor by posting a blurry paparazzi image of Tom wearing his 'I heart TS' vest. He wrote: 'Join me in welcoming the biggest T. Stark fan of them all to Instagram! @twhiddleston. Yes, that's definitely what the "T.S." stands for.'

But what everyone wanted to know was would Tom and Taylor follow each other on social media? And they did.

* * *

Due to work commitments the honeymoon period finally came to an end and Hiddleswift were forced to spend time apart. After a few weeks Tom boarded Taylor's private jet to visit her on Rhode Island, bringing with him piles of gifts. But soon afterwards cracks appeared to be developing in the relationship. *US Weekly* reported the couple had been arguing about spending too much time apart.

'There was so much going on so it was hard making their schedules work, and they were upset they couldn't see each other,' revealed a source.

Then on 6 September 2016, just before the Emmys, where Tom was up for an award as Outstanding Lead Actor for *The Night Manager*, the relationship ended.

On the red carpet for the event, on 18 September, Hiddleston was asked whether he and his ex were still friends.

'Yes, yes, we are,' he insisted.

Rumours were circulating that Tom had wanted Taylor to accompany him to the event, appearing on the red carpet and making their relationship public. But she was determined to keep their romance out of the limelight for as long as possible.

According to *US Weekly* it was Taylor who had ended the affair. 'Tom wanted the relationship to be more public than she was comfortable with,' said a source. 'Taylor knew the backlash that comes with public displays of affection but Tom didn't listen to her concerns when she brought them up.'

A source told *The Sun*: 'Taylor completely bought into Tom. He was a refreshing, charismatic bundle of fun, a joy to be with and she was besotted.

'Her pals loved his nature too. She thought he had the whole package and believed it could develop into something more than a summer romance, so she was bewildered by claims it was all staged.

'But it quickly became apparent that his intentions were different to hers – forcing her to cut ties.'

The mystery deepened when shortly afterwards it emerged that in fact it was Tom who had called off the romance. A theatre producer who had worked with him on *Coriolanus* told *Heat Street*: 'The reports are wide of the mark and come as news to all Tom's friends. He grew tired of Taylor, it wasn't the other way round.

'Tom drifted from her and it had nothing to do with her being put off by the publicity. It's more to do with the fact he's a commitment-phobe who gets bored very easily.'

During a Facebook Live interview with *The Hollywood Reporter*, Tom talked about the pressures of being in a celebrity relationship.

'What have I learned about it? I've learned to – I don't know, maybe it's too soon to tell. Um, I've learned that there are many sides to a story, and that sometimes there are a lot of stories out there which are false, and the hardest thing is to try to not let those falsehoods affect your own life. That's what I would say.

'We all live in a world where every phone has a camera and there's nothing new, really, about the spotlight on me. I think that's what happens when you're a public figure.'

Taylor had a reputation for writing songs about her ex-boyfriends, but as she and Tom had decided to remain friends, it seemed unlikely anything would surface.

'Given Taylor's intention for them to remain friends, it's unlikely Tom will get the treatment,' a friend told the press. 'She's frustrated he turned out to be a different person than she originally thought and was disappointed and shocked by his Emmys demand. But it's not like he treated her badly or made her a laughing stock. She'll get over it.'

In the meantime Calvin Harris had chosen to finally talk with GQ magazine about the end of his relationship with Taylor. Earlier, when she was still dating Tom, Calvin had hit out at her after she revealed she was the sole writer of his single, 'This Is What You Came For'.

He tweeted: 'I figure if you're happy in your new relationship you should focus on that instead of trying to tear your ex bf down for something to do.'

But now he'd calmed down: 'It's very difficult when something I consider so personal plays out very publicly. The aftermath of the relationship was way more heavily publicised than the relationship itself.

'When we were together we were very careful for it not to be a media circus. She respected my feelings in that sense. I'm not good at being a celebrity. But when it ended, all hell broke loose.'

* * *

Now Taylor Swift was firmly out of the picture, the media returned their attention to Tom's future as the next Bond. But some sources revealed that his high-profile hook-up had damaged his chances.

'Bond needs an air of mystery – his public romance

with Taylor has made him totally uncastable,' a source told *The Sun*.

Speaking at a panel event in Philadelphia in June 2016, Hiddleston also declared: 'I'm sorry to disappoint you, everybody. I don't think that announcement is coming.'

It had been a rollercoaster few months, but fortunately he had plenty of other projects to distract him.

CHAPTER SEVENTEEN

A NEW PERSPECTIVE

Although Tom had always craved success and recognition, being famous had never been one of his ambitions. It was simply something – an inconvenience even – that came with the acting territory. But being in the spotlight did have its advantages: he realised he had a voice and what's more, people were willing to listen. As a person in a position of public influence, he has said that he feels a moral responsibility to tackle some of the problems facing our planet. There were so many important issues that seemed to slip woefully beneath the radar.

After learning about the work of UNICEF, he signed up as an ambassador, and when the charity invited him to come and see some of the projects they were working on in Guinea, West Africa, he accepted without hesitation.

The night before his trip, he was so excited, he couldn't

sleep. Instead, he uploaded a video onto YouTube, sharing with fans exactly what he intended to take with him. Standing amidst a pile of clothes and cables, he pulled out the essentials – a mosquito net, a head torch, anti-malarial tablets and his laptop, as he planned to keep a diary of his visit. Other items on his packing list included sweets and biscuits – 'I've been told they go down really well with children!' he said.

Once his packing was done, he stayed up clearing his inbox, and then at 4.30am, a taxi arrived to take him to Heathrow. He looked out of the car window and considered the busy, developed world he was temporarily leaving behind. It was January 2013, and London was cold and damp. People were dressed in woollen jumpers and thick coats.

As he boarded the plane he was filled with a mixture of wonder and trepidation, not knowing what to expect. Stopping at Paris to change planes, his journey took six hours. As they approached Africa, he stared out of the window, looking at miles and miles of desert ahead of him. As soon as he landed in Conakry, Guinea's capital, he was bombarded by sights, sounds and emotions hitherto unfamiliar.

'It hits you like a wave. It envelopes you like a rolling fog. It washes over you like the tide. Heat. West African heat. Guinea. It's hot,' he wrote in a field diary for UNICEF.

Most of all, he was struck by the traffic – seemingly chaotic, it had its own unorthodox order.

It was dark when Tom and the UNICEF team jumped

into 4x4s. Only a minute into the journey they stopped. In a car park opposite the arrivals terminal, children were huddled beneath street lamps, reading. 'Some children walk for an hour just to sit on the ground in a car park to read,' explained Julien Harneis, the UNICEF representative in Guinea.

Over a meal of couscous and quiche, watched by wild cats and bats, Harneis filled the actor in on the history of Guinea.

In his field diary Tom pondered on the country's fate: 'Guinea has been blessed with more peace than its neighbours in recent times, and seems to have avoided being drawn into military conflict. But the same principle applies: a poor nation, with a muddled sense of itself, cannot hope to build a structure that nourishes society without literally feeding its inhabitants.'

He was shocked by the poverty. People had nothing, not even enough food to feed their families. Yet he was amazed by their joy and kindness.

'It rearranges your head, truly, and makes you reassess your priorities and your complaints and your perspectives and so I'm very lucky that I've been allowed to see that,' he said.

Though excited by the prospect of a travel adventure, that rush of adrenaline was quickly replaced by heartfelt awe when he met the Guinean residents – especially the children. In a diary article for *Harper's Bazaar*, Tom talked about his visit and the emotional impact it had on him.

'During my first two days, I experienced joy and sadness in equal measure,' he wrote. 'I was delighted, enlightened, and confused.'

The UNICEF team on the ground introduced him to several projects focusing on children. 'I immediately got a real sense of one of the biggest challenges that children face in the country: hunger and malnutrition,' he wrote. 'When a baby doesn't receive the right nutrients in the first thousand days of life, it can irreversibly "stunt" their physical and emotional development. They will grow up unable to realise their full potential, so that even if hunger doesn't take their life, it will almost certainly take away their future.'

At the National Institute of Child Health and Nutrition (INSE) in the Donka Hospital in Conakry, he met doctors and childcare specialists taking care of malnourished children. There were nearly twenty youngsters crammed into one small ward the size of a bedroom, some close to death.

'Their arms and legs were indescribably thin, their cheeks tear-stained, their skin a harrowing, slate-grey,' he recalled. 'Most shocking to me was the speed and urgency of their breathing, asleep or awake, it was uniformly unsettled and uneven. When you see a child struggling so hard simply to breathe, it makes your heart hurt.'

The ward had just one life-support machine and the hospital was in desperate need of equipment. 'I am shown into a room where I find two of the smallest children I have ever seen. One was born with a terrible skin condition, due to a lack of essential vitamin A, the other was born three months premature. The sight of these two children left me speechless. The skin of the first child was as dry as tracing paper,' he wrote in his UNICEF field diary.

'Why?' Tom kept asking himself. The UNICEF representatives explained that one of the main causes of malnutrition was the failure of mothers to breastfeed. Quite often, they too were ill and suffering.

'It wasn't all bad news at Donka,' Hiddleston wrote. 'I met a newborn boy, whose mother had been previously diagnosed with HIV, but the disease had not been passed on to him. He woke up as I was passing by and was full of smiles and curiosity. Unicef supplied the treatment that protected him from being infected.

'It's also important to say that at Donka they have a cure rate of 65%.'

* * *

After the hospital visit the party went on to a circus school called Project Tinafan in the remote villages. It had been set up to accommodate children who may have dropped out of school.

'Tinafan uses training in the circus arts to strengthen their confidence, bolster their interpersonal skills, and help them trust each other. All of this sounds a little dry. As far as I can see, as soon as I open the car door, these children are *dancing*. I hear pounding drums. I see running, jumping, smiling, free-wheeling, cart-wheeling energy rushing towards me. I see fit, strong, smiling athletes, fit to burst. The thoughtfulness brought on by what I had seen at Donka was instantly dispelled by the sheer, thrilling joy radiating from these children,' Tom observed in his diary for UNICEF.

The children performed a show for Hiddleston, emerging from behind billowing curtains in a frenzy of drums and dance.

'I'm not sure what my expectations were, but they were entirely blown out of the water. I must be as honest as I can: these children are world-class performers of astonishing athleticism and grace. The best among them, I later learned, have toured the world with circus troupes. Their performance was explosive and dizzying – acrobatics, human pyramids, trampolining, contortionists – a display of strength, flexibility and precision on a par with, if not beyond, the very best physical performances I have seen in ballet, contemporary dance, or Cirque du Soleil. They performed with raw joy.'

* * *

Back on a 'bumpy road of potholes, red dust and mango trees', Tom continued on a six-hour drive to his next stop, Saramoussayah. They arrived long after dark and were invited to eat with the elders of the community. He copied Julien Harneis in making a display of washing his hands before the meal, eager to emphasize the importance of hygiene. After a dinner of rice, sauce and banana, he joined a women's focus group, led by Dr Mariam Kankanlabe Diallo.

'She, like all women in the Mamou region, dresses in clothes and a headdress of brilliant colour,' wrote Tom. Sat outdoors beneath the stars, they discussed such topics as washing, breastfeeding and vaccinations.

Before bed, Tom would spray himself 'from head to toe with Jungle Formula insect repellent, brush my teeth, say hello to the five huge spiders sharing a room, slip into my mosquito net and close my eyes'.

The following morning the team embarked on a long and dusty drive east, in the direction of the Mali border, to visit some of the most impoverished communities in the country.

'The road is riddled with potholes, with deep trenches on each side, edging incrementally towards the tarmac, as if some terrifying creature from ancient myth had taken a huge bite out of the side,' he wrote. After several hours his limbs were aching from being scrunched up in a vehicle for so long, although driving past taxis full to the brim with passengers, he knew he was in a much more fortunate position.

In this dry, difficult, remote environment, he felt completely cut off from the rest of the world: 'I have no signal on my phone, I have nowhere else to be, I'm cut off from the rest of the world, and all I have are my thoughts and the great conversation of the team for company.

'But of course the period of endurance is finite for me. In a week's time I'll be back in London, able to choose between the tube, a taxi, a car or bicycle to rush around at high speed. For local Guineans, this is life.'

Later that day, he was asked to appear on a local radio station, funded by UNICEF. In the absence of TV and newspapers this was a way for many people to stay informed about important issues affecting their daily lives. Water and sanitation were topics frequently debated.

Hiddleston went on air to thank local people for their hospitality, and to promise he would share his experiences with the rest of the world. Most impressive of all, he managed to do it all in French. He also visited a sanitation project in a remote village called Loppe, where UNICEF had helped build several wells and latrines, ensuring villagers had access to a clean water supply. Good sanitation was also vital to prevent the spread of disease, Tom learned. Diarrhoea, caused by drinking dirty water, was one of the biggest causes of death amongst children.

That same day he also enjoyed 'one of the most uplifting experiences of my journey'. He was invited into the thatched circular hut of a young family with one boy and two girls. In the single room there was one bed, which also served as a table.

Tom was encouraged to hear the mother had managed to breastfeed her children for the first six months of their lives, after learning it was a good thing to do so on the radio. The father had also taught his son to always wash his hands before eating. In this family he found hope for the future.

When it was time for Tom and his team to leave, the

local residents gave him a 'rousing send-off by bursting into song as our convoy of motorbikes rev their engines and rocket off into the low afternoon sun'.

Even though he was in a place so far from home, the actor still managed to squeeze in his fitness routine. At 6.45am one morning, he went for a run along the river with UNICEF's Julien Harneis. Very soon the deserted area would be packed with people washing clothes, cars and even their bodies.

Julien told Tom about one of his greatest achievements, setting up a project for the reintegration of children who used to be in the army. These child soldiers had been forcibly recruited to military camps, and when Guinea had transitioned from military to civilian rule in 2010, they'd been released without any means of subsistence.

Later that day, Julien took Tom to a project where young men and women were learning different skills such as woodwork, welding, plumbing, carpentry and masonry. 'I've never seen craftsmen and women so proud and passionate about their work,' enthused Tom.

Continuing east, he then encountered a place he described in his diary as 'the most remote place I have ever visited'. Just 35km from the border with Mali, Mandiana is a gold centre, filled with mines.

'Unicef nutrition surveys have shown malnutrition in this area is at its worst,' noted Tom with solemnity. There he witnessed several malnutrition checks and also heard about the urgent need for water.

Visiting a hospital, he was saddened by the number of sick children. He felt further away from his home and own sense of reality than ever before. The idea these people had no access to water was beyond comprehension.

*   *   *

One of Tom's final stops was at a school in Kouroussa, east-central Guinea, where he met several children: 'A little girl, in a red-checked school dress and braids in her hair, was so shy and smiley that she couldn't even tell me her name. I must look like an alien to her,' he wrote in his diary.

He even found time to play football with a small boy who ran rings around him 'like Lionel Messi'.

During another school visit, he was amazed at how well behaved the children were: 'It occurs to me that it was never like that when I was at school in England. If the teacher left the room, there'd be a riot. Here, children want to learn.'

He experienced a very positive energy: 'The country has many difficulties, and I have faced them in all their stark reality this week. But to see healthy children, in love with learning, and happy in their play is restorative and invigorating. It gives me a sense of balance,' he concluded in his diary.

*   *   *

Overwhelmed with emotion, Tom came back to London and told friends and family that the UNICEF visit had been one of the most life-changing things he'd ever done.

'A country like this immediately collapses the walls of your imagination and pushes them back by immeasurable distances in opposing directions. It's mind-expanding.

'I feel as though the cardboard box of my own reality has been flattened and blown open. Now I can see the edge of the world.

'Before my visit to Guinea, I knew that global hunger and malnutrition was a problem. But the issue was only academic in my mind. When you've seen malnourished children with your own eyes and their disadvantaged start in life, a moral imperative compels you to act and becomes impossible to ignore,' he wrote in his diary.

He even claimed he would occasionally wrap himself in a mosquito net at night as a reminder of the experience. It had given him a new perspective on our collective responsibility for the state of our world.

'It's a very, very small world now,' he mused. 'There, I made certain connections about the way the world works, and all the ways it doesn't work: connections that I've been in search of for many years.'

But he was well aware of his own limitations: 'I am no saviour. I'm absolutely the last person on the planet who can practically help,' he said.

One of the funniest things he discovered on his visit is that the word 'actor' doesn't exist in Guinea. The closest equivalent he could find was '*griot*', which means 'storyteller'.

As a celebrity with influence he had the power to

change things and he felt compelled to do something: 'It's absolutely possible that we can eradicate hunger from our world.' His duty now was to make people aware of what was happening in West Africa, and to help them to make a difference, he felt: 'What I learned in Guinea is that we are all responsible for the state of our world. The world – and the system by which we trade, share, cooperate and conflict – is clearly not working. We are only as strong as our weakest members.'

* * *

Compelled to do more charity work, Tom signed up to the Live Below The Line initiative. From 7 to 11 April 2013, he would have to live on food and drink costing no more than £1 per day. His intention was to raise both money and awareness for the men, women and children who have no option but to survive on less than £1 per day.

'I took on the challenge of living on £1 a day out of compassion and a desire to understand the constraints and conditions of those less fortunate, who don't have a choice,' he wrote in a diary for *Harper's Bazaar*. 'For me it was about voluntarily experiencing even the smallest fraction of the hunger, as well as the discipline required, to subsist on such a small amount. The world's poorest families, all over the world, face such malnutrition that their growth and development is held back.'

The actor freely admitted he'd never had to live below the line; he had a nice house in London, with running water, gas and electricity. He also knew he'd been fortunate to have a very privileged upbringing: 'My parents had sufficient income not only to feed me regularly and to feed me well, but also to send me to good schools. To state the obvious: education is power. It always has been; it always will be. I've been very, very lucky. It has given me an emotional and physical strength, which anyone who has lived below the line, for a long time, doesn't have.'

He added that it was lucky he'd not been involved in filming any physical action stunt scenes or battle sequences at the time of taking on the challenge. Now he had to think about food in a completely different way; he had to plan, budget and spend frugally: 'I didn't waste a penny, or a crumb. It was a test of mind and willpower. It was a test, simply because I am unused to being hungry. In order to stay within my budget I had to think carefully, and pay more attention when cooking my own meals. I had to cook my own meals and not buy food on the go. When you only have a 1 kg bag of rice, you take care not to burn it. When you only have two eggs per day, you take care to cook them right.'

Funnily enough, at the same time he discovered a new-found passion for cooking and he was grateful for every mouthful. He also realised he had an addiction to caffeine, as for him foregoing coffee was one of the hardest parts of the process. Focusing on simple tasks became extremely challenging as he suffered the effects of withdrawal but after a few days, his head cleared.

'More than anything, I learned that I could not live the life that I have, if I were hungry all the time,' he concluded.

* * *

UNICEF was extremely grateful for the exposure Tom had helped bring to their campaign. In 2015, they invited him to be an official ambassador, and he eagerly accepted the offer.

His next assignment was a ten-day visit to South Sudan in February 2015. He was backing a campaign by UNICEF UK, calling on the British government to prioritise protecting children from violence in crises, and also making a documentary about the effects of civil war and the recruitment of child soldiers.

Ever since declaring independence from Sudan in 2011, the fledgling country had been wrought with political and civil conflict. Major problems started in mid-December 2013, when the President and Vice President had experienced disagreements; cities had since become warzones, and innocent children were suffering immensely.

The day before he was due to fly, UNICEF announced that at least 89 schoolboys had been abducted while waiting to sit their exams, forced to join the militia as boy soldiers.

Three days later, Tom travelled to the village of Wau Shilluk, in the Upper Nile state of South Sudan, where he visited the 'desolate' school. 'The playground was empty, school desks had been overturned and doors were hanging off their hinges,' he wrote in an article for the *Independent* newspaper.

The actor also visited projects where UNICEF were delivering vital water and healthcare to children and helping to rehabilitate many who had been rescued from the militia.

He witnessed one young boy being reunited with his mother for the first time in more than two years. 'His conscription had left emotional scars,' wrote Tom. 'He had seen things a boy of his age should never have to see. He had the far-off stare of a much older man – a depth in his face.'

The trip proved a very emotional and harrowing experience for Hiddleston and left him with many unanswered questions. All around him he had seen evidence of sophisticated weapons but where had they come from? How could a country stricken by so much poverty actually find the funds to buy such things?

'South Sudan is a forgotten war, which strikes children with unforgivable brutality,' he wrote in his diary. 'It's the most dangerous place I've ever been. We were right in the thick of the civil war... The country's been completely torn apart. It's a huge humanitarian crisis.'

* * *

Shortly after returning to the UK, Tom started work on *The Night Manager*. His trip to South Sudan would have a profound impact on the way he chose to play the role of Jonathan Pine. 'I came back from South Sudan having witnessed, first-hand, the violence from which a man like Richard Roper in *The Night Manager* profits,' he told his friend Benedict Cumberbatch in a piece for *Interview* magazine.

During a dinner with John le Carré, author of *The Night Manager* novel, Hiddleston talked about his trip and revealed 'how powerless I felt, how helpless it seemed that this poor young nation and its inhabitants are being torn apart by a civil war'.

'I feel exactly the same. Use it. Use it,' le Carré told the actor, encouraging him to channel that same frustration, fear and anger into his character.

'In a sense, Pine's moral anger belongs to me,' Tom later admitted.

After their meeting, le Carré sent him a long email as well as a first edition of *Seven Pillars of Wisdom* by T.E. Lawrence. 'It was an extraordinary, beautiful thing to give me,' Tom would later say.

He was still struggling to understand the true extent of what he'd witnessed. Never before had he been exposed to something quite so disturbing.

'The world I've grown into at the moment is becoming increasingly more disturbing and unsettling. Everywhere there is inequality, everywhere there is division, and I worry about it. I think everybody does,' he told Benedict Cumberbatch for *Interview* magazine. 'I wish we could be decent to each other. And I've thought a lot about whether

I have a responsibility to stand up for what I believe in because I have a platform, because I have a voice.

'There is a red line where you do have to stand up for these children. They haven't asked for this. I suppose, as someone who's been asked by UNICEF to be an ambassador, I feel a responsibility to stand up for those children. Because nobody is. So I do, and it's a delicate balance because I'm an actor. And yet somehow, we're given these platforms to speak from and I've been very inspired by people who have had the bravery and courage to do that long before me.'

Even if he'd wanted to remain quiet on the subject – he couldn't. More than a moral obligation, he had a pressing drive to help in any way he could. The situation reminded him of a Nobel address given by the playwright Harold Pinter: 'Truth in drama is elusive. You never quite find it, but the search for it is compulsive. Sometimes you feel you have the truth of the moment in your hand and then it slips through your fingers and is lost. But as a citizen you have a duty to ask what is true and what is false,' said Tom. 'I remember watching him [Pinter] deliver that, feeling very inspired.'

* * *

Just over a year later, during a break in filming, Tom returned to South Sudan in November 2016. In mid-December it would be exactly three years since the conflict first started. Sadly, he witnessed a situation more severe than ever. More than 170,000 children had been treated for malnutrition in 2016 alone.

'Everyone I've met has experienced traumatic events that no one – least of all a child – should ever have to go through,' he declared. 'It's heart-breaking to see that after three years innocent children are still bearing the brunt of the conflict. The physical reality is that when fighting breaks out, everybody runs in different directions. Children become separated from their families – from their mothers, from their aunts, from their brothers, from whoever is looking after them – and are immediately vulnerable to psychological and physical abuse, hunger, and forced recruitment as child soldiers.'

Tom travelled north to a displacement camp in Bentiu, where he met children who had escaped violence, recruitment and abuse. He met two brothers who had been separated from their mother and had not seen her for three years but thanks to UNICEF's reunification programme, she had been located and they would soon see her again.

'I've seen things in South Sudan that will stay with me forever. It's the youngest country in the world, a country which should have so much to look forward to, but the conditions those two boys have to live in – a place still torn apart by civil war – are unimaginable. Knowing that they will be reunited with their mother soon is at least a sign of hope in the immense struggle of the people of South Sudan,' he said in his diary.

Tom was also invited to appear as a guest on *BBC News at Ten* to talk about his visit. He explained to newsreader Huw Edwards why he'd decided to go back to South Sudan for a second visit. 'I felt very invested in the fate of the country. I do think it's interesting that it's the youngest nation in the world and so few people know about it. They say "I wish you luck in Sudan," and I say no, no, it's South Sudan.

'The cost of civil war on children has been profound and I wanted to go back and see what had changed.'

He went on to detail exactly what those developments had been: 'The outbreak of fighting in July has changed the area of danger. When I went last time, the northern part of the country was where the most dangerous risks were for everybody. Because fighting broke out on 7 July in the capital city Juba, the entire eastern and western part of the country, and the south on the border with Uganda, is now very dangerous indeed. That was interesting for us because we were staying in Juba. The curfews were 6pm and we couldn't go out. You could feel the edge.'

The actor also admitted there was no question UNICEF needed more funds for projects: 'There's a huge funding gap – no question. There are so many people affected and they have limited resources. It needs greater investment and attention from governments. It needs to be higher on the agenda.'

In every aspect of his life Tom is a very thorough person. He likes to be educated on a topic so he can speak about it with authority. Having an accumulative two weeks on the ground in South Sudan spread across two trips, he felt he'd developed a good understanding of the situation and the action required.

'I've seen extraordinary despair and struggle, but I've also seen the joy of what happens when it works. When children are brought back to their families, I've seen more tears of joy than I've ever seen in my life and that is what's compelling. That's what makes me feel I have to come and talk about it,' he explained.

He went on to appear on several talk shows and current affairs programmes to talk eloquently about his trip, but unfortunately he wasn't quite so articulate during an awards acceptance speech at the Golden Globes in January 2017.

Collecting his award for Best Actor – Mini-Series or TV Movie for his role in *The Night Manager*, he first thanked his cast, crew and agents, then surprised audiences by talking about his experience in South Sudan.

'*The Night Manager* is about arms dealing and there are far too many arms going into South Sudan,' he announced, before regaling an anecdote. 'There's curfew at 6pm every night, because humanitarian aid workers have to be inside so it's safe. One night we were having a bite to eat at the canteen where we were staying. A group of young men and women tottered over to the table and we were all having a "dirty beer".

'There were some Médecins Sans Frontières (Doctors Without Borders) doctors and nurses, and they wanted to say hello because during the shelling the previous month they had binge watched *The Night Manager*. The idea that we could provide some relief and entertainment to people who are fixing the world where it is broken made me immensely proud. I dedicate this to those out there who are doing their best.'

Unfortunately, not everyone was quite so impressed. As TV cameras scanned the audience to capture their reaction, actor Christian Slater was caught rolling his eyes, while both Vince Vaughn and Naomie Harris appeared confused.

Actor Joshua Malina of *The West Wing* and *Scandal* immediately slated Tom on Twitter, saying: 'Thank you to Tom Hiddleston and all actors who dare to perform in projects that are shown in some of the most dangerous parts of the world.'

Users on social media were also less than charitable, accusing him of 'humblebrag' and 'do-good white saviour rhetoric'.

'That was a long story Tom Hiddleston told to pay himself a compliment,' noted one user on Twitter.

'This Tom Hiddleston speech is the final leg of the Taylor Swift Relationship Redemption Tour,' said another.

'Oh my God did Tom Hiddleston just make South Sudan about me?' another observed.

Later that night during the awards ceremony entertainment website *TMZ* confronted Hiddleston about the Twitter furore. He responded by simply saying: 'We've all just got to do our best to help each other out.'

Keen to set the record straight, he posted a message on Facebook: 'I just wanted to say I completely agree that my speech at the Golden Globes last night was inelegantly expressed. In truth, I was very nervous, and my words just came out wrong. Sincerely, my only intention was to salute the incredible bravery and courage of the men and women who work so tirelessly for UNICEF UK, Doctors Without Borders/Médicins Sans Frontières (MSF), and World Food Programme, and the children of South Sudan, who continue to find hope and joy in the most difficult conditions. I apologise that my nerves got the better of me.'

Most of his followers were understanding and sent some reassuring replies.

'I understand what you were trying to say. The internet blows everything out of proportion,' noted one fan.

'You are at least using your platform to bring attention to worthy causes and to a dire situation. It's important to use your public voice for good,' said another.

And it was true – Tom's only intention had been to bring greater awareness to South Sudan but the usually articulate actor had been caught off-guard. Perhaps he had even been overwhelmed by emotion. After all, with his Loki garb set aside Tom Hiddleston is only human.

CHAPTER EIGHTEEN

MOVING ON

Putting relationship woes and slip-up speeches behind him, Tom now had to concentrate on his next big round of whirlwind promotional tours. He had two major blockbuster releases due for 2017, meaning he'd never be far from the limelight.

His first major release was *Kong: Skull Island*, a story inspired by the giant ape that famously scaled the Empire State Building in the original 1933 movie. Set in the 1970s, the film explores Kong's story before he clashes with the mighty Godzilla. In the film, he's the god of a distant island in the Pacific. Hiddleston, who was one of the first stars to sign up to the movie, was cast as Captain James Conrad, a former SAS and elite hunter who would lead a mission against the 100ft monster. The film would be directed by Jordan Vogt-Roberts, best known for

The Kings of Summer (2013), and would also star Brie Larson and Samuel L. Jackson.

When asked by *Entertainment Weekly* what had attracted him to the role, Tom replied: 'I've always loved Kong; he's an icon of cinema. I've always felt affectionate towards him.'

Once again, he was getting the opportunity to star alongside a character he'd watched as a child. Although he was now an adult, the scale and magnitude of the production was still epic – not to mention the size of Kong himself.

'He is magnificent in it. Wow. He's like 100-feet tall,' revealed Tom to reporters.

But it wasn't just the opportunity to live out a childhood fantasy that attracted him, the concept of the film was also extremely appealing.

'Jordan's idea was so brilliant,' he enthused, 'to relocate it in the early 70s at a time when we believed there might be unsolved mysteries.' He also praised the director for contextualising the film within a political climate, weaving in elements of the Vietnam War. Now typical practice for the educated, thoughtful actor, he had managed to identify a deeper intellectual story lurking beneath the movie's shiny blockbuster veneer.

'It was a new take on a familiar icon who could represent the power of myth,' said Tom. 'As a society, and as an individual, we need to be humbled by things that are greater than us. That's why we travel and watch nature documentaries. We're so stunned by the diversity of nature.

'The story tracks different characters on Skull Island as they are awed by something they do not understand. That's a very powerful thing inside a huge, spectacular blockbuster.'

He spent a long time preparing for the role, brushing up on his political history and also his knowledge of the natural world. 'It's so exciting. I've been digging around in some dark material, to be honest,' he revealed to *Collider* in 2015. 'There's something very heroic about my character in *Kong: Skull Island*. He's an adventurer, he's an explorer.'

At the beginning of the shoot, before he was required to film scenes, the actor locked himself away to transcribe quotes from the 1979 film *Apocalypse Now*.

'I wanted all that amazing John Milius dialogue,' he told *Empire* magazine. 'I now have it on my laptop so I can stew in the juices of that material.'

He also drew inspiration from watching David Attenborough documentaries and described his character James Conrad as 'this extraordinary understanding of the natural world, talking about the food chain, the cycle of life, the basic and essential necessity of predators'.

One day, he was discussing the role with director Jordan Vogt-Roberts, and they started talking about Attenborough and his BBC *Planet Earth* series.

'Suddenly there was this character forming who was very hard, someone who is isolated and mysterious,' Tom told the website *The Nerdist*. 'Isolated by his former experience and deeply charismatic, but when you put him face-to-face with the fantastical world of King Kong suddenly you have an amazing outline for a hero.'

Tom had plenty of opportunities to witness nature first hand during filming, as the shoot for *Kong* took place in several exotic locations, including Australia, Hawaii and Vietnam. 'We travelled to these extraordinary locations to the ends of the earth, where nature is at its most beautiful and terrifying,' he enthused. 'The genius of Jordan Vogt-Roberts' pitch was an encouragement to shoot in real places and to make Skull Island out of parts of our planet that are absolutely breathtaking and remote – where you could believe that Kong as a myth could originate.

'Because it was a world where technology is not what it is now and that perhaps mankind might believe there were mysteries in the South Pacific that were still unsolved. There's an organization in the film called Landsat, which uses satellite technology that we're all now familiar with, with applications like Google Earth. *Skull Island* takes place at the very, very early development of that technology. So, the Western governments are already trying to put together, as it were, a God's-eye view of the Earth and there is one place they can't quite figure out. They send a crew of soldiers and scientists to check it out – and well, the rest remains to be seen.'

From very early on Vogt-Roberts had decided it was important to take his cast on location. 'I'm an outdoorsy guy,' he told *Empire* magazine. 'To me it's important to put the actors into tactile places. When you watch *Platoon* or

Apocalypse Now, the environment is a character. We want people to feel the sweat, the humidity of this island.'

One of his favourite locations was Vietnam, where he got to drive a boat through lakes where 'mountains rise up out of the water like skyscrapers' and also wade through swamps although he confessed, 'they don't tell you about the swamp spiders and things that can get inside your wetsuit and nestle in the warm spaces.'

The idea of Kong 'parkouring through this stuff' was very exciting.

Tom also talked of a helicopter 'sweeping through the valley like a ballet dancer' – 'The excitement of that kind of motion around this type of landscape, it feels new.'

'Vietnam was unbelievable,' he told Benedict Cumberbatch in *Interview* magazine. 'I feel so lucky that I got to go with that production, being part of the traveling circus of a big film like that. We shot in Oahu, Hawaii. We shot in Australia. And we shot in Northern Vietnam, in and around Hanoi, Ha Long Bay and Ninh Binh.

'And I think what's exciting about this is that there is landscape in Vietnam that very few people have ever seen.'

* * *

When Tom and the crew landed in Vietnam in early 2016, local residents were overwhelmed with excitement and eagerly welcomed the Hollywood stars. The team gave a press conference in Hanoi, hosted by the U.S. ambassador to Vietnam.

'It was a very big moment for the country,' said Tom. 'A lot of people we met had never seen a production on this scale.'

In terms of infrastructure a good deal of work was required as some areas of Vietnam were simply so inaccessible. 'In certain places we helped build roads so that we could get the camera equipment in four-by-four trucks to and from where we needed to go,' recalled Tom.

Excited locals even turned up to watch some of the scenes being shot – but soon grew tired of the number of takes. 'On the first day, Sam [L Jackson] turned up for a very simple scene with very little dialogue, and there were thousands of people who turned up to watch,' explained Hiddleston to *Interview* magazine. And then after about an hour they got bored and were like, "Oh, this isn't very exciting. Let's go back to what we were doing."'

Playing a former member of the SAS, Hiddleston had to make sure he was in peak physical condition. Fortunately, he'd never shied away from exercise. Even when he wasn't training for a film, he liked to run every morning to stay in shape and keep both his body and mind agile. 'You've got to do something, even if it's just to kick-start the day,' he said. Eschewing gyms, he preferred to run outside in the elements, 'with only my own legs to propel me forward'. The process allowed him to get 'out of my own head'.

'If I run in the morning before work, I feel like I'm ahead of the day. Whatever work I've done in terms of preparation or research or thinking about the scene or the character, it all kind of crystallizes in that moment in the morning. And sometimes I have the best ideas then,' he explained.

While filming *Kong*, he would often get up and break into a sprint. 'We were always outside. I would always be able to just, like, run around and get my blood up if I was feeling sluggish. I'm quite certain I'm not fit enough to be in the SAS, but I've made strides,' he admitted.

'We've had a lot of ex-military on the stunt team, and I've been trained rigorously by those people. I started about three months before filming. A lot of running. A lot of metcon, which is aerobic workout and resistance. And a lot of circuit training to get my stamina up. My character is incredibly resourceful. Like a coiled spring. Highly skilled. There's plenty of running through jungle terrain, rescuing people who need rescuing.'

Although in the early stages Tom didn't want to give too much of the plot line away, he did hint at a romance with Brie Larson's character: '[Conrad's] sort of a '70s hero,' he told movie news site *JoBlo*. 'He's one of those lone cats. He's got edge. A lot of wit. That's partly why I wanted the character to be British. So that chemistry with Weaver (Brie Larson) would have that old Hollywood banter.

'There's a great sort of back and forth about who gets to make decisions. She mocks him in the beginning for being opaque and mysterious. Later on though, Conrad reveals himself to be really handy in a tight spot, and she's really grateful for that... but she won't let him know! And she also has moments of great bravery and courage and action.

That's what I love about it. There's never been a leading female character in a *King Kong* film like we have.'

Perhaps it was the sweat, humidity and bugs; whatever the reason, crew and cast were bonding quickly. Brie Larson even organised a social 'Brie-ked' of go-karting, laser tag and karaoke, when the team had a break between filming in Hawaii.

'Tom sang "Common People,"' she told *Empire* magazine. 'But I started off the whole thing by putting on an instrumental overture from the musical *Cats*. It really weirded everyone out when they came in and it was just cat noises.'

In Vietnam, where the last scenes were shot, Tom, Brie and Samuel L. Jackson became known as 'The Three Vietnamigoes'. When Larson returned from the Oscars, where she'd picked up an award for Best Actress in the film *Room*, the crew pretended to give her the cold shoulder, only later revealing they had a big celebration planned for their dear friend.

* * *

More than anything, Tom wanted *Kong* to be a proper adventure movie in the vein of classics like *Raiders of the Lost Ark* (1981) and *Jurassic Park* (1993), films he'd grown up with. 'I'm a big fan of adventure cinema,' he claimed.

In an article for the *Financial Times* in 2015, he recalled the first moment he set eyes on King Kong: 'As an actor with a passion for the history of cinema, this is a red-letter day for me. I have stared into the eyes of the ape. A tower of power and majesty, standing like a king,' he wrote.

'In actual fact, the lens of a camera locked on to a frame of my eyes, focused intently and intensely into a deep, dizzying, almost hallucinogenic expanse of green screen, with only my imagination as fuel to the fire. But that's what I love about acting. It is, and will forever be, a childlike act of imagining. Sixteen months from now that single shot will sit side-by-side with a shot of an icon of the cinema, from the days when film as an art form was still in its infancy. King Kong is back.'

Conrad and Weaver's (Brie Larson) first encounter with Kong was filmed in Australia. To set the scene, Tom played *Adagio in D Minor*. 'It became an audible presence of Kong,' he told *Empire*. 'It was really cool – it united everyone. The scene will be incredible: out of the fog he appears, and suddenly we're staring into the face of a myth.'

During his scenes he relied on some acting advice the veteran actor Michael Caine had once given him: 'Don't blink, 'cause they'll cut away. And pick which eye you look into: if you go from one to the other, it conveys weakness on film.'

To keep themselves amused, the cast also started sending each other gifs.

'John C Reilly has instructed me in the way of the gif,' said Tom, proudly to *Empire* in early 2017. 'It's fun, because you can take the piss out of yourself. I've been sending people a particularly humiliating dancey one of me.'

Once filming wrapped in March 2016, he was eager to see how audiences would respond to the production: 'The way Jordan Vogt-Roberts has conceived of it, there's something in there which I find very compelling about King Kong as an emblem of the power of nature in some way, and man's relationship to it. I think he's got just brilliant ideas about exploring that. Incredible sequences, a particular context they put King Kong in that you've never see him in before, so I'm really excited.'

Admittedly, press tours and interviews could be tiring, but he was now an experienced pro at doing junkets and dealing with occasionally crafty journalists who might try to get a rise out of him. 'Over the past two months, I have done a great deal less imagining and significantly more talking,' he said in a diary entry for the *Financial Times*. 'During these press tours – a contractual requirement upon actors in the modern age to help spread the word and to drive box office – one hopes, above all else, to represent the director's intentions, to introduce the film, to deepen the audience's understanding of the context in which the film was made, not to take oneself too seriously, and to emerge with one's personal dignity relatively intact.

'Not everybody plays fair. I have learned a whole new set of skills in dodging headline-chasing hot potatoes: those questions designed to elicit a sensationalist answer more likely to drive traffic to a given website.'

* * *

Alongside *Kong: Skull Island*, Hiddleston was also getting set for the release of *Thor: Ragnarok*, the next highly awaited offering from the Marvel stable. He had been extremely discreet about filming, giving very little away about plot lines. Along with his friend Chris Hemsworth, he would also share the screen with his pal Benedict Cumberbatch, who played Doctor Strange. Although he refused to give away too many details, he did drop a few hints to reporters: 'I can't spoil anything for you. I am in no position to question the wisdom of the Marvel's power-that-be, but let's put it this way, Doctor Strange has very intensely, cerebral, time-bending powers. At the end of *Thor: The Dark World*, Loki's on the throne. What happened to Odin? So, maybe Doctor Strange has to help out with that particular conundrum.'

Much of the filming took place in Australia, with director Taika Waititi at the helm. 'I'm having such a good time,' Tom told the website *Comicbookmovie* during an interview very early on in the filming process. 'Taika Waititi is brilliant, and his vision for his Thor film is so full of wit and humor and drama. He's really been so attentive over the screenplay. I'm so excited. It's a hell of a cast. It's got quite a line-up. It's Chris Hemsworth, Mark Ruffalo, Tessa Thompson, and myself. We've got some others coming.'

Those others included Jaimie Alexander, Anthony Hopkins, Idris Elba, Cate Blanchett, Jeff Goldblum and Karl Urban.

It had been three years since Hiddleston had worked the

Loki costume – 'I think I last wore the costume at Comic-Con in 2013,' he revealed to *Interview*. 'It's just been a long time, and to don the black hair and leather and all of Loki's stuff is good fun.'

As a teaser for fans, he and his good friend Chris Hemsworth decided to share a photo from the film set on social media, comparing their characters from the first 2011 film and how they looked now. Chris also posted a photo of the two men dressed in black, sitting in front of a newsstand.

'Just sellin' papers with my mate' read the caption. In the background headlines on various newspapers read 'Has Thor Returned?' and 'Villain Loki Spotted'.

The film was slated for a late 2017 release, with the plot outlined as follows:

> Imprisoned on the other side of the universe, the mighty Thor (Chris Hemsworth) finds himself in a deadly gladiatorial contest that pits him against the Hulk (Mark Ruffalo), his former ally and fellow Avenger. Thor's quest for survival leads him in a race against time to prevent the all-powerful Hela (Cate Blanchett) from destroying his home world and the Asgardian civilization.

New Zealander director Taika Waititi shared more information about his intentions for the film: 'I think the overall sense that I'm trying to give to the audience and what I want the audience to leave the cinema carrying with them is a sense of joy really.'

As with all Waititi's past films, he confirmed he would have a cameo in the movie.

* * *

More comic-book capers were in store for Tom in an adaptation of nineties series *Hard Boiled*, directed by Ben Wheatley, who had worked with him on *High-Rise*. Hiddleston would play Nixon, a deranged tax collector in a near-future dystopian Los Angeles. The project had been in planning since 2011, but had suffered several false starts.

Embracing animation in its truest sense, Tom had also signed up to do *Early Man*, working with Nick Park and Aardman. The project would be a slow one, pencilled in for a January 2018 release.

Billed as a prehistoric comedy, it would be Oscar-winning Wallace and Gromit creator Nick Park's first film in a decade. Tom would voice the 'ridiculously pompous' Lord Nooth, governor of the Bronze Age town and a rival to the film's Stone Age hero, Dug, voiced by Hiddleston's old Eton pal, Eddie Redmayne.

'Tom is a wonderful actor and it's so thrilling to see him bring our comic villain to life with his amazing talent, energy and enthusiasm,' Nick Park told *Empire Online* in October 2016. 'It is a great privilege to work with Tom and I'm so excited to see his character Lord Nooth emerge on screen!'

Tom was equally excited about being involved: 'I have been a fan of Nick Park and Aardman for as long as I can remember, and am incredibly honoured to be working with Nick and the team on this adventure.

'I'm thrilled to be able to breathe some semblance of life into this hysterical villain and to work with Eddie for the first time. *Early Man* made me laugh out loud when I read it. Lord Nooth is larger than life in every respect. I can't wait for audiences to meet him.'

* * *

Given the plethora of projects he had on the boil, it was hard to imagine Tom even had time to breathe. But if ever he felt tired or exhausted, he thought back to the days when he was desperately seeking work. Not that long ago he'd been a jobbing actor, waiting for the phone to ring. He was painfully aware that even if his star was in the ascendant right now, it could easily crash at any point. Such was the fickle nature of Hollywood. And there was no time to sit back and rest on his laurels; he still had so much further to go.

'You never feel you've hit the peak, that's the predicament,' he told *Business Insider* in April 2016. 'I think you can ask any actor or filmmaker, you never feel like the work is done. It's never possible to say, "That's what I feel about the world, I'll go look after the garden now." I think there are always more stories to tell, there's always more complexity in human life to investigate.'

More than anything, his biggest fear was regret: he

never wanted to feel as if he'd let an opportunity pass by. He had to seize every moment and make the most of what he had available.

'I fear looking back and wishing I had done things I hadn't,' he told Benedict Cumberbatch for *Interview*. 'I read this extraordinary article about a book, many years ago, by an Australian nurse who is a specialist in palliative care. It was her job to help people on their way out, to ease their pain. So she spent a lot of time with people in their last days and weeks. And she felt so moved by the accumulated experience, because she heard people say such similar things. Weirdly enough, at the top of the list was, "I wish I hadn't worked so hard".'

Those words rang true with Tom. Even though he was dedicated to his work, it was still important to make time for his friends and family, the people who cared about him most.

At times he was teased for being overzealous and earnest, but in the cynical realm of Hollywood, his emotional honesty was refreshing.

'Enthusiasm can be dismissed as rather Tiggerish,' said Kenneth Branagh to *Esquire* in 2016, when discussing his prodigy and close friend. 'Tom isn't that at all. He's passionate about ideas and art, and actually I think it's a blessing he's not cursed with that kind of enforced sense of "cool" that requires him to be a bit under-impressed, almost as a badge of honour.

'It's a choice,' he continued. 'Not a natural disposition.'

Tom didn't like to be contained by regulations, but in every aspect of his life – work, rest or play – he lived by one rule of thumb: relish every moment.

It was a mantra that promised many more great moments to come.

SOURCES

ABC, BBC, *Belfast Telegraph*, *Business Insider*, collider.com, comicbookmovie.com, *Complex*, craveonline.com, *Daily Mail*, *Daily Star*, *Daily Telegraph*, *Digital Spy*, *E!*, *Elle*, *Empire*, *Entertainment Weekly*, *EOnline*, *ETOnline*, *Esquire*, *Evening Standard*, *Express*, *Financial Times*, *Gizmodo*, *Glamour*, *GQ*, *Guardian*, *Harper's Bazaar*, *Heat Street*, *Hello!*, hitthefloor.com, *Hollywood Reporter*, *Huffington Post*, *Independent*, *Industrial Insider*, *Industrial Scripts*, *Interview*, io9.com, *Irish Examiner*, *Irish News*, *JoBlo*, JustJared.com, *Mail on Sunday*, *Metro*, *Mirror*, MTV, National Theatre, *New York Times*, *Nola*, *Observer*, *People*, *Plymouth Herald*, *Radio Times*, *Reveal*, *Rolling Stone*, *Rotten Tomatoes*, *Sky News*, *The Spectator*, *Sun*, *Sunday Times*, *Tatler*, *Telegraph*, *Time*, *Time Out*, *The Times*, TMZ, UNICEF, urbandictionary.com, *US*,

US Weekly, Vanity Fair, Variety, View London, Vogue, Wall Street Journal, YouTube.

Joss Whedon: The Biography, by Amy Pascale (Chicago Review Press, 2015)

Also thanks to Ystad Tourism Agency and The Graham Norton Show (BBC).